DK EYEWITNESS TRAVEL

TOP 10
SEOUL

MARTIN ZATKO

Penguin
Random
House

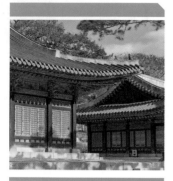

Top 10 Seoul Highlights

The Top 10 of Everything

CONTENTS

Seoul Area by Area

Streetsmart

Within each Top 10 list in this book, no hierarchy of quality or popularity is implied. All 10 are, in the editor's opinion, of roughly equal merit.
   Throughout this book, floors are referred to in accordance with American usage; i.e., the "first floor" is at ground level.

Front cover and spine *South Korea, Seoul, Deoksugung Palace*
Back cover *Bongeunsa Temple in the Gangnam District of Seoul, South Korea*
Title page *Colorful paper lanterns at Bongeunsa Buddhist temple*

Welcome to
Seoul

Although South Korea's capital city is still largely an enigma to the Western world, growing numbers of travelers are beginning to visit to absorb the unique energy of this spellbinding megalopolis. Having reinvented itself as one of Asia's cultural capitals, this is Seoul's time to shine, and with Eyewitness Top 10 Seoul, it's yours to explore.

Though now relentlessly modern, Seoul retains an impressive amount of history, boasting no fewer than five ancient dynastic palaces, of which **Gyeongbokgung** and **Changdeokgung** are the most popular. Sandwiched between them is **Bukchon Hanok Village**, a stretch of achingly beautiful wooden housing, while just to the south is charming **Insadong**, an area filled with traditional restaurants and tearooms, quirky galleries, and tiny museums.

After this peek back in time, turn to contemporary Seoul. Areas such as shop-filled **Myeongdong**, cosmopolitan **Itaewon**, swanky **Gangnam** (yes, that Gangnam), and party-hard **Hongdae** are as modern as they come, all pulsating with a heady mix of neon and K-pop. And if this all gets too much for you, the city has a national park right on its doorstep. Sprinkled with temples and dominated by soaring peaks, **Bukhansan National Park** is a short ride away from central Seoul on one of the world's best subway networks.

Whether you're coming for a weekend, a week, or even a month, our Top 10 guide will give you the lowdown on Seoul's best offerings, from Buddhist festivals to barbecued beef, and from trinkets to traditional tea. Specialized sections enable you to head off the beaten path or simply seek out what's free to do, while seven easy-to-follow itineraries help you to make the best use of your time. Throw inspiring photography and detailed maps into the mix, and you have the essential pocket-sized travel companion. **Enjoy the book, and enjoy Seoul.**

Clockwise from top: **Changdeokgung palace, The Secret Garden, Bongeunsa temple, Bukhansan park mountains, Smiling Buddha, Banpo floating island, temple decorations**

Exploring Seoul

Seoul may be quite unlike any city you've ever been to – a giant, teeming, and potentially bewildering place. Planning is essential if you are going to make the best use of your time in South Korea's fascinating capital. Here are some ideas for two and four days of sightseeing in Seoul.

Gyeongbokgung's throne room houses a beautifully decorated folding screen.

Key
— Two-day itinerary
— Four-day itinerary

Two Days in Seoul

Day ❶
MORNING
Take a tour of **Gyeongbokgung** (see pp12–13), the oldest and grandest of Seoul's five palaces, and see historical artifacts in the National Palace Museum.

AFTERNOON
Spend your afternoon sipping traditional tea in characterful **Insadong** (see pp16–17) and trinket-shopping in **Ssamziegil** market (see p59), before visiting **Jogyesa** temple (see p72).

EVENING
Walk up the small peak of **Namsan** (see pp24–5) before sunset, and see Seoul light up in bright neon lights.

Day ❷
MORNING
After coffee in **Samcheongdong** (see p33), stroll through the winding lanes and wooden houses of **Bukchon Hanok Village** (see pp32–3).

AFTERNOON
Admire the famous old gate of **Dongdaemun** (see pp22–3), before repairing to earthy **Gwangjang Market** (see p23) for a meal.

Four Days in Seoul

Day ❶
MORNING
Start by exploring **Gyeongbokgung** palace (see pp12–13), the National Palace Museum of Korea and the National Folk Museum.

AFTERNOON
Get a glimpse of traditional Seoul in **Bukchon Hanok Village** (see pp32–3), then hit the designer boutiques in **Samcheongdong** (see p33) and visit the **Kukje Gallery** (see p14).

Day ❷
MORNING
Take tea in characterful **Insadong** (see pp16–17), and go shopping for traditional souvenirs – **Ssamziegil** market (see p59) is a good spot.

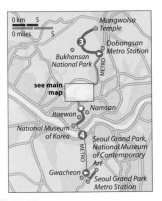

Bukhansan National Park is a fascinating expanse of wilderness within the city limits of Seoul.

Insadong is the place to go to acquire typical Korean souvenirs, like these masks.

AFTERNOON

Enjoy a relaxing afternoon in the quiet Duamdong area (see pp30–31) including a visit to the **Whanki Art Gallery** (see p30).

Day ❸

MORNING

Head for the hills of **Bukhansan National Park** (see pp28–9), a short subway ride from central Seoul. Walk the Wondobong trail, aiming for **Mangwolsa** temple.

AFTERNOON

Take your pick of two palaces – intriguing **Changgyeonggung** or splendid **Changdeokgung** (see pp26–7) – then make your way to **Dongdaemun** for dinner (see pp22–3).

Day ❹

MORNING

Head south to the suburb of **Gwacheon** (see pp34–5) to enjoy Seoul Grand Park, Seoul Land amusement park, and the National Museum of Contemporary Art.

AFTERNOON

Come back to Seoul for a look around the **National Museum of Korea** (see pp20–21), then head to fashionable **Itaewon** (see pp86–9) for a meal or coffee.

EVENING

Walk or take the cable car up **Namsan** peak (see pp24–5), to witness a Seoul sunset in the most spectacular place possible.

Top 10 Seoul Highlights

Traditional pavilions at
Changgyeonggung palace

🔟 Seoul Highlights

Despite being one of the world's most modern cities, Seoul has many historic sights. Its two oldest and most splendid palaces – Gyeongbokgung and Changdeokgung – date from the turn of the 15th century, as does Dongdaemun, Seoul's oldest existing city gate. The neighborhoods of Insadong, Bukchon, and Buamdong offer a taste of dynastic-era Korean life, while a trip to the nearby city of Gwacheon will give you a break from the frenetic pace of Seoul.

Gyeongbokgung

The halls and pavilions in the "Palace of Shining Happiness", a focal point of the city since its completion in 1394, are superb examples of Buddhist decoration. Its museums are among the best in the land *(see pp12–13)*.

Insadong

Seoul's most popular tourist neighborhood is also one of its most traditional, with its zigzagging lanes crammed with restaurants, superb galleries, and craft stores *(see pp16–19)*.

National Museum of Korea

Korea's rich, colorful history is best explored in this gigantic museum, a repository of treasures from the various dynasties that have held power on the peninsula over the last 2,000 years *(see pp20–21)*.

Dongdaemun

Named after the ancient "Great East Gate" that still stands at its center today, this district is now famous for its huge open-air market – offering everything from Korean food to silk *(see pp22–3)*.

Namsan **5**

Rising from Seoul's very center and topped by the distinctive N Seoul Tower, this mountain is the ideal place from which to survey the city. Its tree-lined trails are great for a gentle hike (see pp24–5).

Changdeokgung and Changgyeonggung **6**

These UNESCO World Heritage-listed palaces offer what many visitors to Asia look for: great wooden architecture, manicured gardens, and the timeless air of dynasties long past (see pp26–7).

Bukhansan National Park **7**

Temples, hermitages and Confucian academies stud this national park's myriad hiking trails, which wind up toward a series of granite peaks (see pp28–9).

Buamdong **8**

Although not far from Central Seoul, this area exudes the air of a provincial town. Its galleries, restaurants, cafés, and stores can easily take half a day to explore (see pp30–31).

Bukchon Hanok Village **9**

Korea's traditional wooden houses – hanok – are rare nowadays, but the narrow, hilly lanes of this charming area are lined with many pristine examples (see pp32–3).

Gwacheon **10**

Just south of Seoul is the city of Gwacheon, home to many day-trip possibilities. Choose from a theme park, a zoo, a contemporary art museum, a Confucian shrine, and the capital's largest tract of parkland (see pp34–5).

🗔 10 ⭐ Gyeongbokgung 경복궁

Taejo, the first king of the Joseon dynasty, selected Seoul as his inaugural capital in 1392, and the building of Gyeongbokgung – the "Palace of Shining Happiness" – was completed just two years later. This majestic structure has been of prime importance ever since, and served as the royal residence until 1910. The myriad halls and gates dotting the complex are a riot of color, though in true Confucian style any opulence is balanced by nature – in this case, the pine-covered mountains which rise to its north.

1 Gwanghwamun
This imposing southern gate (**below**) is one of Seoul's main landmarks. Destroyed and rebuilt several times through the ages, the current gate was unveiled in 2010, after four years of reconstruction.

2 The Front Courtyard
During the day, visitors buy tickets for the palace here. In the evening, it is perhaps Seoul's best spot for viewing the sunset – the grand palace fading against the setting sun makes for a striking sight.

3 Stonework
An assortment of sculptures – both traditional and contemporary in design – can be found just north of the National Palace Museum of Korea. This is a grassy area, ideal for picnicking.

4 The Northern Sector
In this little-visited sector of the complex, many buildings which were destroyed in the Japanese occupation of Korea have been reconstructed. They exude a timeless air and are worth a visit.

5 Gyeonghoeru
This pavilion (**below**) was constructed during the reign of King Taejeong (1400–18), who hosted banquets and State meetings here. Located in the middle of a lake, it is accessed via a stone bridge with ornately carved balustrades.

Map of Gyeongbokgung

8 Geunjeongjeon Hall

This two-tiered structure was the former throne room **(below)** of the palace. Inside, a folding screen is placed behind the Joseon throne, featuring the sun, the moon, and five mountains on a blue background.

9 Parujeong

One of the most distinctive buildings in the complex, this two-storied octagonal structure was built in 1888 and used as a library by King Gojong. Interestingly, its design is more suggestive of the Chinese Qing dynasty than Joseon-era Korea.

6 National Palace Museum of Korea

Over 45,000 artifacts from Seoul's five palaces, spanning the 500-year reign of the Joseon dynasty, are housed here. Look out for statues, scrolls, and fragments of the original palace woodwork

7 Gangnyeongjeon Hall

Built in 1395, this hall was used as a bed chamber by several Joseon kings. Rebuilt in 1995, it is decorated with original dynastic furnishings.

A TURBULENT HISTORY

Given what it has been through, it is something of a miracle that Gyeongbokgung still stands. The first major issue was the disastrous fire of 1553, followed by the Japanese invasion of the 1590s which saw much of the palace razed to the ground. All but 10 buildings were destroyed during the Japanese occupation of Korea (1910–45), which was followed by the devastating Korean War. Major reconstruction has been underway since 1989, and half of the palace's buildings are already back in place.

10 National Folk Museum

This museum has an assortment of original dynastic clothing **(below)**, as well as hands-on displays that are popular with kids.

NEED TO KNOW

MAP L1 ■ 161 Sajikro ■ www.royalpalace.go.kr

Open Mar–May, Sep & Oct: 9am–6pm; Jun–Aug: 9am–6:30pm; Nov–Feb: 9am–5pm; last adm 1 hour before closing ■ Closed Tue

Adm W3,000 (adults), W1,500 (7- to 18-year-olds); The palace is also accessible with the Integrated Palace Ticket (see p112)

■ Free English-language tours are offered outside the Gwanghwamun ticket

booth at 11am, 1:30pm, and 3:30pm every day. Tours last between 60 and 90 minutes.

■ There is a restaurant within the National Palace Museum, and a café inside the National Folk Museum.

Gyeongbokgung Museums and Galleries

The ultra-modern Kukje Gallery

1 Kukje Gallery

국제 갤러리

MAP L2 ■ 54 Samcheongno
■ 735 8449

Kukje ("international" in Korean) is an appropriate name for this gallery, which has done more than any other to cultivate ties between the Korean and Western art worlds. Big-name artists from abroad usually see their art land here when undertaking a show in Korea.

2 Artside Gallery

아트사이드 갤러리

MAP K2 ■ 33 Tonguidong
■ 725 1020

In the trendy Seochon neighborhood, this gallery is of major importance to Seoul's art scene, not least due to its connections with Beijing – offerings in the large basement hall are a mix of local works and Chinese superstars or stars-to-be.

3 Daelim Museum

대림미술관

MAP K2 ■ 21 Jahamunno 4-gil
■ 720 0667

This modern gallery started life in the city of Daejeon as an exhibition space for local photography. Though this is still the main focus,

the artistic boundaries have since extended into other spheres. Their roster includes at least one world-famous name each year.

4 National Museum of Modern and Contemporary Art

국립 현대 미술관

MAP L2 ■ 30 Samcheongno
■ 2188 6000

This is the third, and newest, wing of the MMCA – the other two are in Deoksugung palace (see p77) and Gwacheon (see pp34–5). The focus here is more educative than at the other venues, with films, exhibitions, performances, and programs tailored to give local youths a dose of culture. It's centered on the Madang space, which functions as a Korean version of the Turbine Hall in London's Tate Modern.

5 Arario Seoul Gallery

아라리오 갤러리 서울

MAP L1 ■ 84 Bukchonno 5-gil
■ 541 5701

The spacious halls at this well-designed venue suit larger-scale sculptures and paintings. There is a sister gallery in Shanghai, making this a great place in which to take the pulse of the art scene across the Yellow Sea. It also has ties with the Indian and Southeast Asian art worlds – the end result is really rather exciting.

Installation at the Arario Gallery

6 Gallery Hyundai

갤러리 현대

MAP L2 ■ 14 Samcheonno
■ 2287 3500

This is Korea's oldest commercial gallery, deservedly milking all the respect that comes with such a claim. Unlike many galleries in the area, the focus is mostly local, with a particular bias toward artists active from the early to mid-20th century – years of conflict that spawned artists with plenty to say.

7 Gallery Factory
갤러리 팩토리

MAP K2 ■ 15 Jahamunno 10-gil
■ 733 4883

Once a gallery for cutting-edge local art, this is now more of a hub for local artistic endeavor, and a must-visit for anyone interested in cultivating connections with, or simply understanding, the Seoul art scene. However, the gallery still puts on exhibitions of experimental work, making it rewarding even for the casual visitor.

The avant-garde Gallery Factory

8 Project Space Sarubia
씨루비아 나방

MAP K1 ■ 158-2 Changseongdong
■ 733 0440

This gallery started life in the 1990s, as one of Seoul's only true cafés – the Sarubia Coffee Shop, a haunt of local artists. Some of those artists

decided to up sticks and create a local space for experimental art, blurring the boundaries of music, dance, film, architecture, and more.

9 Jean Art
진화랑

MAP K2 ■ 7-38 Tonguidong
■ 738 7570

The first thing likely to strike you on your approach to this complex is one of Japanese artist Yayoi Kusama's famous pumpkins, lurking behind a large window. As well as contemporary art from across the sea, there is plenty of local fare to get your teeth into – as well as great tea in a hidden upstairs café.

10 National Palace Museum
국립 고궁 박물관

MAP L1 ■ 12 Hyojaro ■ 3701 7500

Part of Gyeongbokgung *(see pp12–13)*, this museum has a superb collection of paintings, scrolls, metal- and woodwork from all five of Seoul's former royal abodes. The undoubted highlight is Ilwolobongdo, a folding screen featuring the sun, moon, and five mountain peaks on a blue background – this, and similar screens, were once used as backdrops to the throne.

Gallery, National Palace Museum

TOP 10 ⭐ Insadong 인사동

Seoul's most popular tourist district, and with good reason, Insadong is by far the most interesting and quintessentially Korean place in the city to shop or eat. Most of this area is made up of narrow, winding alleys known as *golmok*, which are a delight to wander about in. These lanes are filled to the brim with small charming galleries, restaurants, tearooms, and trinket shops, of which some are housed in traditional wooden *hanok* buildings.

① Unhyeongung
Seoul's unofficial sixth dynastic palace, Unhyeongung **(below)** was denied the title as it was never occupied by a king. Though not as striking as the others, it is charming and has a tranquil atmosphere, making it worth a visit.

④ Jogyesa
Seoul's most prominent temple **(right)** is the headquarters of the Jogye order, Korea's primary Buddhist sect. The main hall is a fantastic example of the country's colorful and immaculately painted temple decorations.

② Sunday Visits
Traffic is barred from entering Insadonggil on Sundays, making it a good day to visit. In warmer months, you might even see a parade or a musical display here.

③ Insa Art Center
Insadong's largest gallery is also the most interesting – exhibitions change weekly.

⑤ Ahndamiro
This excellent Italian restaurant is a notable exception in Insadong - a neighborhood well known for its traditional Korean eateries. Fast, friendly service and authentic dishes are the foundation of this unexpected venue.

⑥ Tapgol Park
Named for a 15th-century stone pagoda from a Buddhist temple that was once located here, this park hosted a 1919 protest against Japanese occupation. Bas reliefs **(left)** depict scenes from the independence movement.

⑦ Story of the Blue Star
A local favorite, this tiny restaurant serves mountain food and interesting *makgeolli* (a type of rice wine) infusions. The menu is written in Korean, in a calligraphic style, on the walls.

Map of Insadong

AVOID-HORSE ALLEY

Jongno, in the heart of Insadong, has been Seoul's most important road since ancient times. Aristocrats, known as *yangban*, would glide along the road on their horses and, as they passed, commoners were required to prostrate themselves before them. Eventually, thoroughfares hidden from *yangban* view were created. Pimatgol, a side-street just north of Jongno, and running parallel to it, literally translates to "avoid-horse alley."

⑨ Yetchatjip
This tearoom's claim to fame are the dozen or so small birds that fly around it freely. The herbal infusions it offers are also excellent.

⑩ Balwoo Gongyang
The best of Seoul's vegetarian "temple food" restaurants, Balwoo Gongyang **(left)** peers out over Jogyesa – the ideal setting. Dishes are served in the wooden bowls from which the restaurant takes its name.

⑧ Ssamziegil
Popular with Korean youth and tourists, this handicrafts market is essentially a single path that spirals up through four floors. In addition to shops, the complex has a few good restaurants on the upper level *(see p59)*.

NEED TO KNOW
Map M3

Unhyeongung: 114–10 Unnidong; 766 9090; open Nov–Mar: 9am–5:30pm Tue–Sun; Apr–Oct: 9am–6:30pm Tue–Sun; adm

Insa Art Center: 188 Gwanhundong; 736 1020; open 10am–7pm daily; adm

Jogyesa: 55 Ujeonggukro, Jongnogu; 768 8660 or 8661 (for tourists)

Ahndamiro: 15-2 Gwanhundong; 730 5777; open 11:30am–11pm daily

Story of the Blue Star: 17-1 Insadong 16-gil (exit 6 of Anguk station, then turn left between the parking lot and the police station); 734 3095; open noon–3pm & 6–10pm daily

Ssamziegil: 38 Gwanhundong; 736 0088; open 10am–8:30pm daily

Yetchatjip: 2F 196–5 Gwanhundong; 722 5332; open 10am–11pm daily

Balwoo Gongyang: 71 Gyeonjidong; 733 2081

■ The best time to visit Insadong is just before sunset when it is at its least crowded.

TOP 10 Insadong Souvenirs

Visitors shopping for jewelry at a street market stall in Insadong

1 Pendants and Jewelry

Insadong is a great place for jewelry – a stroll around the bustling Ssamziegil complex (see p17) will reveal a variety of shops selling styles from traditional to contemporary. Visitors should also look out for stores selling tiny silk pendants – these make attractive and inexpensive souvenirs.

2 Tea Sets

There is a tremendous range of tea sets in Insadong, and they are among the most popular purchases by visitors. Head to Insadonggil for the inexpensive ones, or to shops such as Yido Pottery (see p74), Kwang Ju Yo, and the Korea Culture and Design Foundation Gallery (see p74) for designer fare.

Tea pot

3 Name Chops

Some art-supplies shops also sell name chops. Made from marble, jade, and other stones, these are still used across East Asia today in lieu of a signature. If requested, these can be inscribed with foreign names, in either Roman or Korean characters.

4 Traditional Clothing

The strikingly colorful *hanbok* is the national dress of Korea. Insadong has several tailors who can make this outfit, although commissioning one may be a little expensive. It's a better idea to check out one of the stores in the area selling contemporary styles; try Sami (see p74) for wearable options.

5 Art Supplies

Insadong's area has long been a favorite with local artists, and has dozens of art-supplies shops that cater to their needs. Apart from high-quality paints and paper, these shops also sell a range of excellent brushes.

Colorful paint brushes for sale

6 Rice Cakes

Rice cakes play an important role in the life of Koreans – they form part of many meals, and are used as table decorations during holidays and coming-of-age ceremonies. Bizeun (see p74) sells ready-to-eat rice cakes as well as takeaway souvenir packs, and the many rustic stores around Fraser Suites (see p114) sell cheaper versions of the same.

Handmade paper fans

You can buy entire rolls of this from the art-supplies shops, but non-artists will doubtless be more interested in items made with *hanji* – including lanterns, hand fans, calligraphic scrolls, and figurines.

Shop selling Buddhist regalia

7 Buddhist Regalia

The most important Buddhist temple in the city, Jogyesa (see p16) lies on the western fringe of the Insadong area. There is a clutch of shops near the temple, selling traditional Buddhist paraphernalia. Although these are intended for the benefit of worshipers, the clothing, incense, and bronzeware are sure to interest visitors as well.

8 Handmade Paper

Koreans are proud of their local paper; known as *hanji*, it is usually made from mulberry leaves.

9 Paintings

Insadong is packed with art galleries, and a few places offer visitors the chance to purchase local art. While the basement of the Ssamziegil complex (see p17) is a good place to go looking, most of the area's smaller, more independent galleries are also worth a visit.

10 Pottery

Korean pottery has been admired since the time of the Three Kingdoms, and is popular to this day. A couple of shops, located just north of the main Insadong area, are superb places for pottery shopping – Yido Pottery (see p74) has a fantastic range of earthenware. Also worth visiting, the smaller, classier Kwang Ju Yo shop is down the road (see p74).

Traditional Korean pottery in an Insadong shop window

🔟 ⭐ National Museum of Korea 국립중앙박물관

Korea's National Museum is, by far, the country's most important repository of historical artifacts. Once housed in the grounds of Gyeongbokgung palace, it moved in 2005 to a state-of-the-art facility on land previously owned by the US Army. This treasure trove gives visitors a chronological tour through Korean history – from the Paleolithic to the Three Kingdoms period, and then through the Silla, Goryeo, and Joseon dynasties.

Ten-Level Pagoda

The undisputed centerpiece of the museum is this gigantic Buddhist pagoda **(right)**, first erected in 1348 during the Goreyo dynasty (918–1392).

2 Baekje Ornaments

Kings of the Baekje dynasty (18 BC–AD 660) had a penchant for golden accessories in a style resembling Art Nouveau **(above)**. The headgear found inside the tomb of King Muryeong in Gongju, the capital of the Baekje dynasty, is a good example.

3 Metal Type

A Korean Buddhist document, *Jikji Simche Yojul*, printed in 1377, the world's first book printed with movable type – beat Gutenberg's Bible by 78 years. The museum has pieces of the original metal type on display.

4 Comb-Pattern Pottery

Dating back to 5,000 BC, these earthenware jars, decorated with a zigzag pattern, were used to store and carry food. These are among the earliest Korean archaeological finds.

Key to Floorplan
- Third floor
- Second floor
- First floor

5 Pensive Bodhisattva

In a room of its own on the third floor, this finely worked figurine is made of bronze and was cast in the early 7th century.

6 Silla Jewelry

The Silla dynasty unified the Korean peninsula around 660. Their jewelry, similar to that of the Baekje dynasty, is best exemplified by decorative crowns and earrings **(right)**.

7 Buddhist Paintings

The Buddhist painting room has a series of elaborate and colorful Buddhist scrolls and folding screens from the Goryeo and Joseon periods.

THE MANY NAMES OF SEOUL

Seoul has had many names. Known as Wiryeseong under the Baekje kings (18 BC–AD 660), its name changed to Hanju in Silla times (660–918) and to Namgyeong under the Goryeo dynasty (918–1392).

It was known as Hanseong, then Hanyang, under Joseon rule (1392–1910), and as Keijo under Japanese occupation (1910–45).

10 Kim Hong-do's Genre Paintings

Genre paintings by Kim Hong-do (1745–1806) are revered by museum curators. These simple illustrations **(below)** perfectly evoke the clothing, gestures, and practices of the time.

8 Dynastic Pottery

Dynastic-era pottery **(above)** fills several halls on the museum's third floor. Korean artisans worked with porcelain and celadon, but some of their techniques remain a mystery even today.

9 Joseon's Basic Code of Laws

During the Joseon dynasty, Korean society became highly Confucian in nature. A series of documents showcases the rituals that were common in society at that time.

NEED TO KNOW

MAP C4 ■ 168–6 Yongsandong ■ 2077 9000 ■ www.museum.go.kr

Open 9am–6pm Tue, Thu & Fri, 9am–9pm Wed & Sat, 9am–7pm Sun. English-language tours of the museum start at 10:30am and 2:30pm

■ Pick up pamphlets and leaflets from the information desk in the main lobby.

■ The museum has several options for refreshments – there's a trendy café up the stairs from the main entrance, a tearoom at the opposite end of the first floor, a good restaurant overlooking the lake outside the museum, and a convenience store for snacks.

🔟⭐ **Dongdaemun** 동대문

An elaborately painted, two-tiered structure that once marked the eastern perimeter of Seoul, Dongdaemun literally means "Great East Gate." The city may have expanded but the gate, dating from 1398, is still here despite being wrecked by fire, restored, and rebuilt again in 1869. Today it represents an interesting mix of renovation and reconstruction. The gigantic market area that has developed around Dongdaemun is one of the most fascinating places in all of Korea.

① **Dongdaemun**
This gigantic ornamental gate was known as Heunginjimun in the past **(above)**. It now sits at the heart of the city district that goes by the same name.

② **Cheonggyecheon**
Starting just south of Gwanghwamun station, this stream **(below)** runs for 5 miles (8 km) below street level. Pedestrians love the path alongside it.

③ **Lantern Festival**
Seoul puts on spectacular lantern festivals along the Cheonggyecheon stream, featuring a mix of traditional designs and animal floats.

NEED TO KNOW
MAP D2

Lantern Festival: held mid-May each year (dates may vary)

Gwangjang Market: open 9am–6pm (opening hours may vary from store to store)

Dongdaemun Market: shops: open 8am–6pm daily; food court: open 7am–7pm daily

■ There are a number of excellent restaurants in the area, including Woo Lae Oak and Samarkand *(see p81)*. For a simpler meal, make your way to Gwangjang Market.

5 Gwangjang Market

Gwangjang consists of two intersecting covered arcades, with innumerable side alleys that are home to fabric stores. The stalls and cafés **(left)** are fascinating places in which to eat.

6 Dongdaemun History and Culture Park

Previously a baseball stadium, this landscaped area around the Design Plaza has been turned into a cultural space.

SEOUL UNDER CURFEW

Today, Dongdaemun gate is bang in the center of the city, and the market around it buzzes with activity day and night. However, during the dynastic era, this great gate marked the far eastern edge of the city, and the area around it was shut at sundown at the tolling of a bell. This gave its name to Jongno (Bell Street), which lies west of the gate *(see p17)*.

7 Dongdaemun Design Plaza

To the south of Dongdaemun gate, this urban development project **(above)**, designed by the late architect Zaha Hadid, houses exhibition spaces, plus shopping, business, and relaxation facilities.

Map of Dongdaemun

8 Dongdaemun Market

To the south of the gate is a series of malls **(right)**. Popular with locals and visitors alike, they sell inexpensive copies of branded goods.

9 Russia Town

The area has been given this name due to the Cyrillic signs on display there. However, most traders here are from Mongolia and Uzbekistan.

4 City Walls

Seoul's giant gates were once part of a wall that encircled the city. Follow the roads up to Naksan Park for lovely views of a remodeled section stretching north of Dongdaemun.

10 Furniture District

Step outside Euljiro 4-ga subway station's south-facing exits and enter a district where dozens of shops sell nothing but home furnishings.

📷10 ⭐ Namsan 남산

Mountains make up most of Korea's landmass, so it is no surprise to find one right in the middle of Seoul. Namsan, a 860-ft- (262-m-) high peak, once marked the city's southern edge. Nowadays it is home to several interesting sights: the iconic N Seoul Tower sprouts from Namsan's summit; its slopes are a veritable maze of pleasant hiking trails, while on the foothills you will find a traditional performance hall and some enchanting wooden *hanok* buildings.

N Seoul Tower
Seoul's best-known landmark stands like a gigantic needle atop Namsan's summit **(right)**. Its observation deck offers superb views, and there are many dining and entertainment options inside.

② Teddy Bear Museum
Located in the N Seoul Tower, this is one of Seoul's more curious museums. As the name suggests, it is dedicated to teddy bears and there are all sorts on display.

③ Namsan Gugakdang
Situated in the park area behind Namsangol, Namsan Gugakdang is Seoul's most traditional performance hall – *gugak* means "national music" in Korean. Performances are diverse, but are always interesting to watch.

④ Mongmyeoksan Beacon Towers
These stone towers **(left)** date back to the Joseon era. They were part of a larger series of towers used to relay warnings across the peninsula.

NEED TO KNOW
MAP D3 ■ 100–177 Hoehyeondong 1-ga ■ 3455 9277

N Seoul Tower: open 10am–11pm Mon–Thu & Sun, 10am–midnight Fri & Sat

Teddy Bear Museum: open 10am–10pm Mon–Thu & Sun, 10am–11pm Fri & Sat; adm

National Theater: 2280 4114

Namsan Cable Car: open 10am–11pm daily; adm

Ohreumi elevator: open 9am–11:30pm daily

Namsangol Hanok Village: 2264 4412; open Apr–Oct: 9am–9pm Wed–Mon, Nov–Mar: 9am–8pm Wed–Mon

■ Namsan's summit can be crowded around sunset; try coming for sunrise instead.

■ There are snack bars in and around N Seoul Tower and near the lower terminus of the cable car. The N Grill restaurant is inside the N Seoul Tower.

5 National Theater

Located on Namsan's eastern flank, this is among Korea's foremost performance venues. It is also an entry point for the mountain's most popular walking path.

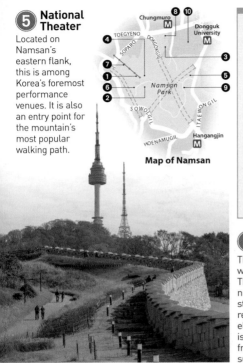

Map of Namsan

SMOKE SIGNALS

During the Joseon era, Koreans used smoke signals to communicate, and Namsan was the fulcrum of a nationwide network of chimneys used to signal warnings. Depending upon the perceived level of threat, between one and five beacons would be lit; the signal would then be copied at beacons on successive mountainsides, all the way up to the coasts and the Chinese border.

7 Namsan Cable Car

The cable car is a fun way to ascend Namsan. Though its lower terminus is a fair way above street level, it can be reached via the Ohreumi elevator – the entrance is just a short walk away from the Myeongdong subway station.

6 Locks of Love

The top of Namsan has countless "trees" covered with padlocks **(below)**, which symbolize eternal love. Couples buy a lock, write a message on it, and then attach the lock to one of the trees and throw away the keys. The spot is extremely popular with both visitors and locals.

8 Namsangol Hanok Village

This cluster of wooden buildings **(above)** are genuine abodes from the Joseon dynasty that were relocated here from other parts of Seoul. You can see how Seoul used to look, and also take part in simple traditional games.

9 Walking Paths

Namsan's slopes are covered with walking paths, but it is possible for visitors to lose their way; descending from the summit, in particular, can be tricky.

10 Dongguk University

Located at the foot of Namsan, this university is one of the most prestigious educational institutions in South Korea.

TOP 10 ★ Changdeokgung 창덕궁 and Changgyeonggung 창경궁

Two of Seoul's five royal palaces, Changdeokgung and Changgyeonggung, are separated only by a wall. Though their names sound similar, there is plenty to distinguish between the two. Completed in 1412, Changdeokgung is the older of the pair, and the best-kept of Seoul's palaces. Changgyeonggung, on the other hand, completed in 1483, is a humbler palace and is connected by footbridge to Jongmyo, a park-like compound that serves as a shrine for the kings of Joseon.

1 Donhwamun
Originally built in 1412, Changdeokgung's huge, two-tiered main gate **(above)** was burned down during the 1592 Japanese invasions, rebuilt in 1607, and finally restored in 1609.

2 Geumcheongyo
A 600-year-old granite bridge, this is one of the few survivors from Changdeokgung's original construction. The animal faces carved into various points of the bridge are typical of the early Joseon period.

3 Changgyeonggung Greenhouse
To the north of Changgyeonggung is a Victorian-style greenhouse. Built in 1907, it is now home to over one hundred species of plants.

4 Injeongjeon
Although ravaged by fire several times, the throne room at Changdeokgung **(left)** remains truly spectacular. It holds a replica of a folding screen that the Joseon kings used as a backdrop to their thrones.

5 Huijeongdang
This hall in the royal palace of Changdeokgung was used by several kings of the late Joseon period and, somewhat incongruously, features Western-style carpets, floorboards, and chandeliers.

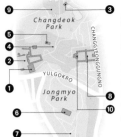

Changedeok
Park

YULGOKRO

Jongmyo
Park

**Map of
Changdeokgung and
Changgyeonggung**

6 Jongmyo

This shrine (below) has two halls that house the "spirit tablets" of all Joseon kings. Every ruling king came by five times a year to pay his respects. A re-creation of this ceremony, known as Jongmyo Daejae, takes place each May (see p62).

7 Jongmyo Park

A small area outside Jongmyo's entrance that is favoured by elderly Korean men who meet to play board games.

**PALACE OR
THEME PARK?**

Changgyeonggung's greenhouse predates the Japanese occupation by three years, but it became a symbol of the oppression that followed. In an attempt to sully the dignity of Korea's royal line, the Japanese turned the palace into a theme park of sorts, with the greenhouse as a focal point. While it is viewed as an unacceptable slight against the nation today, the theme park was enjoyed until the early 1980s – almost 40 years after the end of occupation.

8 Munjeongjeon

In 1762, Prince Sado – heir to the throne – was killed at his father's behest at Munjeongjeon, a gate protruding from the Changgyeonggung palace walls.

9 The Secret Garden

Created as a place of pleasure for kings, this garden (left) is centered on a stunning lotus pond.

10 Myeongjeongjeon

This hall in Changgyeonggung is the smallest in any Seoul palace. It was supposed to be the living quarters of the dowager queen.

NEED TO KNOW

MAP P2

Changdeokgung: 110–360 Yulgokro 99; 762 8261; open Feb–May, Sep & Oct: 9am–6pm, Jun–Aug: 9am–6:30pm, Nov–Jan: 9am–5:30pm; closed Mon; adm W3,000

Secret Garden: open from 10am; closed Mon; adm W2,000; eng.cdg.go.kr

Jongmyo: adm W1,000

Changgyeonggung: 2–1 Waryongdong; 762 4868; open Feb–May, Sep & Oct: 9am–6pm, Jun–Aug: 9am–6:30pm, Nov–Jan: 9am–5:30pm; closed Mon; adm W1,000 (adults), W500 (7- to 18-year-olds)

■ Changdeokgung can only be visited as part of a guided tour, including monthly night tours. The Integrated Palace Ticket (see p112) is valid for the palaces and Jongmyo.

TOP 10 ★ Bukhansan National Park 북한산 국립 공원

Seoul is a rarity among world capitals, in that it has a national park within the city limits. The park is split into distinct northern and southern sections, although both offer the same charms – a series of mountain trails, freshwater streams, rippling tendons of rock, granite peaks, and a clutch of functional Buddhist temples and hermitages. The trails are ideal – simple enough for hiking novices, yet steep enough to provide a good workout.

Jaunbong (3)

At a height of 2,430 ft (740 m) above sea level, Jaunbong **(right)** is the highest peak both along the ridgeway and in the park's northern section.

4 Northern Ridgeway

A ridge trail runs for 6 miles (9 km) from the Uidong entrance to Wongaksa temple – start early to complete it within the day. On the way there are three major peaks, many smaller crests, and a few Buddhist temples.

1 Streams and Waterfalls

The park's long ridge trails are surrounded by valleys, many of which feature stream-side walking trails and small waterfalls. The streams **(above)** are perfect to dip your feet in after a hike.

5 Cheonchuksa

Perhaps the most distinctive of Bukhansan's temples, Cheonchuksa **(below)** is also one of the oldest, dating to 673 BC. It is located under Seoninbong, a granite peak.

2 Dobong Seowon

Confucian academies, known as *seowon*, were once the backbone of the educational system but were restricted to the aristocrats. This relic, near the Dobongsan park entrance, is a remnant of that time.

EDUCATION IN THE JOSEON ERA

During the Joseon period, education was largely restricted to the children of the *yangban*, the aristocratic elite, who studied in private Confucian academies known as *seowon*. Tests were notoriously hard to pass – even the writer Yi Hwang (1501–70), one of Seoul's most revered scholars, took four years to pass his preliminary government exams, and another seven to finally become a civil servant.

⑥ Mangwolsa

Located between the Northern Ridgeway and a subway station, Mangwolsa temple is the park's focal point for hikers. This small beautiful temple dates back to the 7th century. On the way up, follow the Wondobong valley trail, which features a few freshwater springs.

Map of Bukhansan National Park

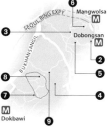

⑨ Rock Climbing

Bukhansan's southern section, particularly the area around Insubong **(below)**, is becoming popular with rock climbers. This is best suited to climbers with experience; see the Korea on the Rocks website for details.

⑧ Baekundae

At 2,746 ft (837 m), Baekundae **(left)** is the park's high point and part of the Bukhansanseong Trail. It is no surprise that the views from here are breathtaking.

⑦ Bukhansanseong Trail

In the early days of the Joseon dynasty, a fortress wall **(below)** was built in Bukhansan to protect Seoul from invaders. Renovated many times since, its contours form a delightful hiking trail.

⑩ Mountain Food

In Korea, it is customary to eat *pajeon* (pancakes) after a hike. If you prefer mountain fare, many restaurants serve *sanchae bibimbap*, a take on *bibimbap* (see p46).

TOP 10 ⭐ **Buamdong** 부암동

During the early years of Korea's economic boom, Buamdong and the neighboring Pyeongchangdong district were considered Seoul's most luxurious places to live – one reason for the presence there of many large houses and ornate villas. Young Seoulites visit in droves on weekends, punctuating their strolls with visits to the area's quirky cafés and bars.

Bugaksan ①
Once Seoul's northern boundary, this mountain is home to restored portions of the fortress walls **(right)**. Security is high here, so carry your ID.

② Sanmotoonge
In a city filled with high-rises, it's astonishingly hard to find a café with a view. Head to Sanmotoonge, where outdoor tables afford amazing vistas of the Bukhansan mountain range to the north.

④ Whanki Art Gallery
Kim Whanki was part of the Parisian avant-garde movement in the 1930s, and he brought Western ideas and techniques back to Korea. This superb gallery **(left)** is devoted to his works.

⑥ Inwangsan
The Buamdong area is also a starting point for the many trails up rocky Inwangsan, one of Seoul's most important religious mountains **(below)**.

⑤ Dining
Buamdong has become very trendy and is popular with couples on a date. You will find Italian food on most menus, but Jaha Sonmandoo's *(see p73)* dumplings, usually served in casseroles, are more appropriate to the scenery.

③ Jahamun Gate
This large gate once marked the northern end of Seoul. Its splendid paint and stonework stand out within its natural setting.

7 Gana Art Gallery

South Korea's largest gallery is tucked into mountain foothills. The building's sprawling halls help ensure there is plenty of space to appreciate the gallery's exhibits.

8 Typography

The neon signs seen nearly everywhere in Seoul are absent here. Typography comes in the old painted and metal forms – look out for the simple whitewash-on-brick logo of Hanyang Ricecake Shop.

FROM PYONGYANG WITH LOVE

An idyllic place today, Bugaksan mountain holds a dark secret. In 1968, it was the scene of an assassination attempt on the life of then-president Park Chung-hee. A team of North Korean commandos had crossed the border and made their way down to Seoul; by the time they were apprehended, they were just half a mile from the presidential abode. Almost 100 were killed as the team tried, in vain, to head back to the DMZ (see p64).

10 Baeksasil Valley Walk

This mostly flat, child-friendly trail takes around 2 hours, and on the way you'll pass by picturesque streams, picnic places, and a couple of temples.

Pyeongchangdong Villas 9

Buamdong's neighboring district, Pyeongchangdong sports a few large *hanok* villas **(right)** that were built in the old days before the advent of high-rise apartments.

NEED TO KNOW

MAP C1

Sanmotoonge: 97–5 Buamdong; 391 4737; open 11am–10pm daily

Whanki Art Gallery: 210–8 Buamdong; 391 7702; open 10am–6pm Tue–Sun; www.whankimuseum.org

Gana Art Gallery: 97 Pyeongchangdong; 720 1020; open 10am–7pm daily; www.ganaart.com

▪ Come to Buamdong during the week if you can. It is a tremendously popular target for weekend jaunts, and crowds can dilute the area's appeal.

Map of Buamdong

TOP 10 ⭐ Bukchon Hanok Village
북촌 한옥 마을

Bukchon is an island of tradition in modern Seoul. *Hanok*, the wooden houses that once blanketed Korea, have now largely been replaced with concrete towers, making Bukchon a living museum of historic Korean architecture. You'll see *hanok* aplenty here; while most are functioning homes, some have been converted into charming cafés, tearooms, and galleries.

Views **1**
The maze-like alleys of the Bukchon neighborhood **(right)** are a delight to wander. Though there are eight officially designated "Viewing Spots," stroll around and you will doubtless come across your own splendid vista.

2 Choong-Ang High School
At the top of the Bukchon area is this prestigious school **(above)**. Built in 1937, it is one of Seoul's most beautiful Colonial-era buildings designed in a Western style. A functioning school, it can only be visited on weekends.

3 Hanjeongsik
In the alleys near Anguk subway station are several *hanok*-style restaurants serving *hanjeongsik* – traditional Korean meals.

4 Changdeokgung Views
Head to the sports field behind Choong-Ang High School and you'll be afforded a unique, and rather breathtaking, view of the off-limits northwestern corner of Changdeokgung palace **(below)**. The largest hall you can see is the Sinseonwonjeon, which was used to house official portraits of the kings of Joseon *(see pp26–7)*.

6 Samcheongdong

Adjoining Bukchon is Samcheongdong **(left)**. Run-down for decades, this revitalized neighborhood is now bursting with funky cafés and restaurants, and is also a great place for a stroll.

7 Night Visits

The Bukchon area is hugely popular with locals, and during the daytime it can become a little crowded. Visit at night, when the area is almost deserted, and the *hanok* houses look even more spectacular.

8 Samcheong Park

Samcheongdonggil – the main road in the Samcheongdong area – goes up to Samcheong Park, a pleasant space. Paths lead from here to Seoul's old city wall.

9 Tearooms

Insadong, to the south, may have a wider variety of tearooms, but experiencing a traditional tea in Seoul's most traditional area is a delight. Meander through Bukchon's winding alleyways, and stop at one for a break.

5 Pottery

The Bukchon area offers some wonderful shopping opportunities, particularly if you are interested in buying high-quality ceramics **(above)** – Kwang Ju Yo and Yido are the pick of the bunch *(see p74)*.

Galleries and 10 Museums

As well as large galleries, the area also has a sizable number of small, private art spaces and museums, most displaying wonderfully quirky artifacts **(right)**.

HANOK HOUSING

Most *hanok* have a central, dirt courtyard. Around this are arrayed several rooms, each with sloping roofs of slate tiles stacked on plaster and wooden beams. Between vertical beams of wood stand sturdy walls of plaster and mud, covered on the inside with sheaves of mulberry paper. This paper is also used to line the floors, varnished to a yellow glaze and heated from beneath by wood fires.

NEED TO KNOW

MAP M1 ■ All sights here are within walking distance of Anguk subway station (line 3, exits 1 and 2).

■ There are plenty of *hanok* cafés and tearooms in Bukchon Hanok Village – try Books Cooks (see p55) for English tea and scones, LN (see p75) for coffee, or Cha Masineun Tteul (see p50) for traditional Korean tea.

■ Several information booths dot the area. The ones uphill from Anguk station's exit 2 and the Arario Gallery are the most accessible.

TOP10 ⭐ Gwacheon 과천

Seoul is one of the world's most densely populated cities, and parkland is at a premium here. Visitors staying for longer than a few days might wish to escape the crowds and enjoy some greenery. The neighboring city of Gwacheon makes the perfect destination; it is centered on Seoul Grand Park, a mountain-backed swath of land which also features an art gallery, a huge zoo, and one of Korea's biggest theme parks.

1 Gwacheon National Science Museum

Exhibitions at this museum are quite futuristic (below). There is also a planetarium and, outside, a sculpture-studded walking space.

2 Gwacheon Hyanggyo

In the dynastic era, aristocrats studied at government academies known as *hyanggyo*. This particular one lies in the foothills of Gwanaksan.

4 Seoul Grand Park

This gigantic green area, centered on a lake (above), spreads up into the surrounding mountains. In good weather, you could spend the whole day here.

5 Cheonggyesan

This mountain lies to the back of Seoul Grand Park and some of its many hiking trails start in the park itself. Hiking enthusiasts can try scaling the 2,027-ft- (618-m-) high summit.

6 Seoul Zoo

A part of Seoul Grand Park, this is one of Asia's largest zoos (below). It is home to animals such as zebras and giraffes, and there is also a petting zoo.

Map of Gwacheon

3 National Museum of Contemporary Art

Affiliated to the eponymous facility in Deoksugung palace (*see p77*), this museum owns over 8,000 artworks from Korea and abroad.

8 Equine Museum

This small museum inside the Race Park complex is dedicated to horses, and has a number of paintings and sculptures featuring the animals **(left)**.

BETTING AND GAMBLING IN SEOUL

The Seoul Race Park in Gwacheon is one of the few places in South Korea where it is legal for locals to gamble. However, plenty of small-scale betting takes place in other forms, the most popular of which is a local card game known as *hwatu* – older Koreans can often be spotted playing this game outdoors. The small, decorative cards used to play *hwatu* can be purchased from any convenience store, and they also make great souvenirs.

10 Gwanaksan

Rising up to the west of Gwacheon, this small mountain has many hiking trails. The easy 90-minute walk up to the 2,073-ft (632-m) summit is recommended.

7 Seoul Race Park

This race park is one of few places in South Korea where gambling is legal. Races take place 10am–5pm on weekends and you can also bet on horses running in Jeju and Busan – the other courses in the country.

Seoul Land 9

A massive amusement park **(right)**, Seoul Land offers visitors over 40 rides – the Sky-X, a 180-ft- (55-m-) high free-fall ride, is the most famous. The complex also has walking trails and a series of mock-European buildings.

NEED TO KNOW

MAP G2

Gwacheon National Science Museum: open 9:30am–5:30pm (last entry by 4:30pm); adm W4,000; www.scientorium.go.kr

Seoul Grand Park & Zoo: open Mar–Oct: 9am–7pm daily, Nov–Feb: 9am–6pm daily; adm W2,000–W5,000

National Museum of Contemporary Art: open Mar–Oct: 9am–6pm Tue–Sun, Nov–Feb: 10am–5pm Tue–Sun; adm

Seoul Land: open 9:30am daily, closing time varies from 6–10pm; adm W18,000 (a day pass is available for W32,000); www.eng.seoulland.co.kr

■ Seoul Grand Park and Seoul Land are popular retreats. For a little peace and quiet, try to visit them early in the day or late in the afternoon.

■ There are many shops selling snacks in and around Seoul Land and Seoul Grand Park. For long hikes, carry water and snacks with you.

The Top 10
of Everything

**Striking modern architecture of
the Dongdaemun Design Plaza**

Moments in History

1 18 BC: Founding of Baekje

King Onjo founded the Baekje dynasty, one of Korea's famed Three Kingdoms. Though the exact location of Wiryeseong, Baekje's first capital, remains unknown, experts agree that it lay within the boundaries of present-day Seoul – most likely near what is now Jamsil.

Early portrait of King Taejo

2 1394: Seoul Becomes a Capital

King Taejo made Seoul the first capital of Joseon (1392–1897), a dynasty he had founded two years earlier. His far-reaching influence is still felt today – the palace of Gyeongbokgung was built within a decade, as were much of the city walls and their colossal gates.

3 1450: Death of King Sejong

King Sejong's main legacy was *hangeul*, the Korean alphabet – invented during his reign as a means of enabling the education of the common man. However, widespread literacy was only achieved by the 20th century. To this day, Sejong is revered as one of Korea's greatest leaders.

4 1590s: Japanese Invasions

The last decade of the 16th century saw two major invasions of Korea by Japanese armies, led by General Hideyoshi. Most of the fighting took place on Korea's southern coast, though much of Seoul was also destroyed in the process.

5 1762: Murder of Prince Sado

This royal murder occurred in Changgyeonggung, when, at the behest of King Yeongjo, Prince Sado – his son and heir to the Joseon throne – was left to die inside a rice casket.

6 1910: Japanese Annexation

After Japan formally annexed Korea in 1910, systematic attempts to eradicate Korean identity were made (including the renaming of Seoul as "Keijo") until Japan was forced from power at the end of World War II.

7 1950: Korean War

After World War II, Korea was divided into a Soviet-backed north and a Western-backed south. The inevitable civil war kicked off in 1950, with Seoul changing hands four times before the 1953 armistice. A peace treaty has not yet been signed.

Soldiers during the Korean War

President Park Chung-hee

 1962: Park Chung-hee Takes Control of Korea

Military strongman Park Chung-hee seized power of South Korea in a coup d'état, and officially became president the following year. Though often authoritarian, Park's rule saw the country develop from a war-scarred backwater into an industrial powerhouse.

Ben Johnson at the 1988 Olympics

 1988: Seoul Olympics
Some of the most memorable moments of the Seoul Summer Games were quite unusual: doves burning to death on the lighting of the torch; Ben Johnson's 100-m world record and subsequent disqualification; and Greg Louganis winning the diving gold medal after hitting his head on the board.

10 2002: FIFA World Cup
Seoul hosted the opening game of football's World Cup, an event co-hosted with Japan. South Korea became the first Asian country to play in the World Cup semifinals, and was defeated 1–0 by Germany.

TOP 10 KINGS OF JOSEON

1 Taejo (1392–98)
Founder of the Joseon Kingdom, he helped shape today's Seoul with a series of grandiose projects.

2 Taejeong (1400–18)
Taejo's fifth son inherited the throne after murdering or exiling other contenders, including his own siblings.

3 Sejong the Great (1418–50)
Revered king who ushered in an age of invention, including the Korean alphabet.

4 Seongjong (1469–94)
This king continued Sejong's legacy by encouraging invention and experimentation.

5 Yeonsangun (1494–1506)
Notorious tyrant who launched purges of intellectuals. His love for a male court jester was portrayed in the 2005 film *The King and the Clown*.

6 Seonjo (1567–1608)
Infamous for not protecting the country during the 1590s, Seonjo even had the eventual savior, Admiral Yi Sun-shin, arrested and tortured.

7 Sukjong (1674–1720)
A skilled politician, Sukjong managed to enhance Joseon's prosperity despite intense factional infighting.

8 Jeongjo (1776–1800)
The son of Prince Sado, he reformed Joseon in a turbulent period.

9 Gojong (1863–1907)
Crowned king as a child, first Gojong's father, and then eventually his consort, ruled the country on his behalf.

10 Sunjong (1907–10)
The final king of the Joseon dynasty, whose brief rule ended with Japan's annexation of the country.

Artwork depicting King Jeongjo

TOP10 Museums and Galleries

National Museum of Korea

1 National Museum of Korea
국립 중앙박물관

Korea's flagship museum of history and art is spread over three themed floors. The first floor has exhibits dating back to the Three Kingdoms period and beyond; the second focuses on paintings and calligraphy; and the third holds pottery and Buddhist sculptures (see pp20–21).

2 National Palace Museum of Korea
국립 고궁박물관

Located in the Gyeongbokgung palace grounds and accessible on the same ticket, this museum exhibits an assortment of stonework, calligraphic scrolls, painted eaves, and other treasures from Seoul's five palaces (see p13).

3 Leeum, Samsung Museum of Art
삼성미술관 리움

This gallery is split into two main halls designed by architects Mario Botta and Jean Nouvel. One houses several forms of traditional Korean art, while the other features contemporary works from Korea and abroad (see p87).

4 Kukje Gallery
국제 갤러리

Kukje is Korean for "international", so it is easy to guess what this gallery focuses on. Since its opening in 1982, Kukje Gallery has been showcasing works by the likes of Joseph Beuys, Damien Hirst, and Cy Twombly, as well as helping popularize Korean art overseas (see p14).

5 National Museum of Contemporary Art
국립 현대 미술관

This museum has two superb locations – a Colonial-era structure in Deoksugung palace (see p77), and the leafy surroundings of the Seoul Grand Park (see p34). Head to the former if pressed for time, and the latter for a day trip (see p79).

Expansive hall at the National Palace Museum of Korea

8 Owl Art & Craft Museum
부엉이 미술 & 공예 박물관
MAP D1 ■ 27–21 Samcheongdong
■ 3210 2902

Displays here include sculptures, figurines, and paintings of owls; the museum is truly representative of the Bukchon area's quirky galleries.

9 Gana Art Gallery
가나 아트센터

Designed by Jean-Michel Wilmotte, the same architect responsible for the award-winning Incheon International Airport, this extensive gallery displays a variety of exhibits, including paintings and video art (see p30).

Seoul Museum of Art

6 Seoul Museum of Art
서울시립미술관

This building once housed the Supreme Court of Korea. Remodeled in 1995, the gallery has exhibited works of masters such as Mark Rothko, Henri Matisse, and Vincent van Gogh, and its modern interior is suitably splendid (see p79).

7 Whanki Art Gallery
환기미술관

This gallery is dedicated to the works of Kim Whanki, a famous abstract artist whose work was inspired by the three cities he lived in – Seoul, Tokyo, and Paris. It also organizes exhibitions featuring similar work by contemporary Korean artists (see p30).

10 Seoul Museum of History
서울역사박물관

The collections in this museum give not only a glimpse of the Seoul of the past, but an understanding of its transformation into a world-class city. It also hosts art exhibitions from time to time (see p78).

Artifact in the Seoul Museum of History

Modern Seoul

1 Jongro Tower
MAP M4 ▪ 4 Jongro 2-ga

Seoul's metamorphosis from the Brutalist designs of the 1980s can be said to have started with the renovation of Jongro (or Jongno) Tower in 1999. Uruguayan architect Rafael Viñoly endowed the tower block with an eye-catching "floating platform," supported by three latticed columns.

2 SK Building
MAP L4 ▪ 11 Eulji-ro 2-ga

Impressive as the Jongro Tower renovation was, it offered little insight into Seoul's future layout. SK Building, on the other hand, caused little fuss when completed a year later, but has since gone on to become the city's architectural reference point – many newer neighbors have aped its wonky steel-and-glass approach.

3 Cheonggyecheon
MAP M4

Completed in 2005, the renovation of the Cheonggyecheon stream involved tearing up the elevated highway and market areas which had covered the stream for decades. Seoulites expressed deep concerns at the cost – but millions pop by each year for a walk by the stream *(see p22)*.

The renovated Jongro Tower

Incheon International Airport

4 Incheon International Airport
MAP F2 ▪ 2851 Unseodong, Incheon

Incheon International Airport, which opened in 2001, proved a vast improvement on its functional predecessor, Gimpo Airport. All flowing lines, gentle curves, and open spaces, it has gone on to scoop a whole host of international airport awards.

5 Times Square and D Cube City
MAP A5 ▪ Times Square: 442 Youngdeungpodong 4-ga; D Cube City: 662 Gyeonginro

Created in an effort to revitalize the city's southwestern corner, these two projects are, perhaps, a sign of Seoul to come – a mix of office space, malls, parkland, bars, and restaurants, each topped with a five-star hotel.

6 Samsung d'light
MAP E6

Not all signs of modernity are architectural – take Samsung, a Korean company which has revolutionized television and mobile phone design. While you will see the latter in the hands of most of your fellow subway passengers, you can also take a peek at Samsung designs of the future in d'light, Samsung's superb showroom in Gangnam district *(see p100)*.

⑦ City Hall
MAP L5

Completed in 2012, Seoul's new City Hall sits proudly at the center of the city next to its predecessor, which was built in 1926 by the Japanese. Although said to resemble temple eaves in design, the new building, soaring above the old, seems almost menacing in appearance *(see p80)*.

⑧ New Districts
Seoul has made a habit of ripping up whole swaths of the city for the sake of modernization. A few areas have become quite spectacular – witness the ultra modern surroundings of Gangnam station, or the even newer districts going up in Yongsan and Incheon's Songdo island.

⑨ Floating Islands
MAP D5 ■ www.floating island.com

"Floating" in the Han River, these three artificial islands opened for business in 2011. Although primarily

The Han River's Floating Islands

built to house conventions, performance venues, restaurants, and the like, their park areas are open to the public and are great for a stroll.

⑩ Dongdaemun Design Plaza
MAP D2 ■ www.ddp.or.kr

Designed by late Iraqi-born architect Zaha Hadid, this huge complex was built on the site of an old baseball stadium – and, evidently, a Joseon-dynasty garrison, remnants of which form part of a museum added to the original designs *(see p23)*.

Dongdaemun Design Plaza and Culture Park

Off the Beaten Path

Stalls at Tongin Market

1 Tongin Market
MAP J1 ■ Tongindong 6
■ 9am–6pm Mon–Fri, 9am–1pm Sat

At this quirky market, customers exchange W5,000 for retro coins, then use these to buy snacks from the various stalls. The most popular with local visitors – families and youngsters – is *deokbokki*, a dish of rice cake and spicy sauce.

2 Gilsangsa
MAP D1 ■ 323 Seongbukdong
■ 3672 5945 ■ www.kilsangsa.or.kr

Jogyesa *(see p16)* is by far the most visited temple in Seoul, but it's not truly representative of Korean Buddhism in design or feel. If you have time, try hunting down this gorgeous little temple up in the northern hills. Despite being a relative newbie (having opened in 1997), its location and atmosphere are particularly conducive to meditation – the House of Silence is a section dedicated to this practice.

3 Walking Routes

MAP C1/D2/M1 ■ Bugaksan: open 9am–5pm daily (last entry 3pm)

You can join many of northern Seoul's sightseeing dots on a series of delightful trails, the best of which runs north from Dongdaemun gate *(see p22)* toward Samcheongdong *(see p33)*. You can even continue to the charming Buamdong area *(see pp30–31)* via the small peak of Bugaksan, though you'll need your passport for the Bugaksan section, since it's near the presidential abode and somewhat sensitive.

4 Jeongdonggil
MAP K/L5

Starting by City Hall and running past the southern wall of Deoksugung palace, this is – though

Intricately carved pagoda and bell at the Buddhist temple of Gilsangsa

Tree-lined Jeongdonggil

not car-free – one of Seoul's most pleasant walking streets, lined with ginkgo trees and the occasional low-key restaurant or café. The former Russian legation, near the western end of the street, is a suitably undervisited spot.

5 Seochon
Though just a stone's throw west of Gyeongbokgung, this earthy area remained almost entirely off the radar until 2014, when a few trendy restaurants (such as Jeon Daegamdaek, *see p73*) opened up in and around the local courtyard houses. The area hasn't been fully gentrified yet, however, and you will still see traditional sights such as simple laundrettes and old ladies selling beans. For now, this is perhaps the most pleasing neighbourhood in all of Seoul.

6 Owl Art & Craft Museum
Perhaps the most eccentric of the Bukchon area's many museums, this place draws together artsy owls from across the globe – more than 2,000 in total, with some embossed on plates or vases, others standing as figurines, and more printed onto folding screens (*see p41*).

7 Mongmyeok Sanbang
MAP D3 ▪ Namsan ▪ 318 4790
▪ 11am–9pm daily
Tucked away alongside the Namsan hiking trail (*see p87*), this delightful,

part-hidden venue functions as both a restaurant and a tearoom. The interior is pleasant enough, but even better – with cooperative weather – is the open area out back, where you'll be able to eat delectable *bibimbap* or chat over some herbal tea, against a dramatic backdrop of trees.

8 Inwangsan
The trails of Bukhansan National Park (*see pp28–9*) can get uncomfortably crowded, especially on weekends – queuing to reach the top of a mountain is not everybody's cup of tea. While not a national park, Inwangsan (*see p71*) is closer to Seoul, offers better views of the city, and is rarely crowded. It is also a focal point for the indigenous religion – turn up at the right time and you may witness a Shamanist ceremony.

A traditional boat on Yangsu-ri island

9 Yangsu-ri
MAP G1
This small, bucolic island lies east of the center, at the confluence of two rivers. These combine here to form the Hangang, which flows through Seoul, though there's little big-city atmosphere here – think rice fields and river views (*see p65*).

10 Gyeonghuigung
Seoul's "forgotten" palace (*see p78*) tends to get overlooked in favor of its more illustrious counterparts, but those who choose to visit will benefit from the relative absence of crowds. The various buildings here are beautiful in their own right, and it's an easy walk from Insadong or City Hall.

🔟 Culinary Specialties

Meat ready for barbecuing

5 Samgyetang
This delicious broth is made with ginseng-stuffed chicken, and is healthy even by the sky-high standards of Korean cuisine.

6 Bibimbap
Literally meaning "mixed rice," this simple dish has religious origins, with the main ingredients of the dish corresponding to the colors linked with Buddhism locally – white for rice, yellow for egg, red for spice, green for vegetables, and blue for meat.

1 Barbecued Meat
Cooking your own meal in a restaurant may sound like a chore, but in Korea it's a lot of fun. Meat houses, or *gogi-jip,* dole out rounds of meat to customers, who finish the job on charcoal fires set into the tables. The most popular meats include *galbi* (beef or pork ribs) and *samgyeopsal* (pork belly), and all are served with free side dishes.

2 Jeon
Korean pancakes, or *jeon,* come in many varieties. The most common are *bindaeddeok* (mung-bean), *gamja jeon* (fried potato patties), and *haemul pajeon* (seafood).

3 Hanjeongsik
A must-try for those visiting Korea, these are traditional meals in which the whole table is blanketed with dozens of side dishes – a colorful mix of vegetables, meats, and fish served with rice, broth, and more.

4 Seafood
Unfamiliarity makes most foreigners wary of trying Korea's excellent seafood. The solution: head to Noryangjin Fisheries Wholesale Market (see p93), point at what you want, then take it up to an upper-floor restaurant, where your purchase will be prepared for you.

Colorful bowl of *bibimbap*

7 Naengmyeon
A cold but spicy dish made with buckwheat noodles, *naengmyeon* is similar to Japanese *soba.* It's actually a North Korean specialty; many of Seoul's best *naengmyeon* restaurants, including Woo Lae Oak (p49), were started by northerners who crossed the border during the Korean War.

Naengmyeon, a North Korean dish

Kimchi, **a pickled vegetable side dish**

8 Kimchi

The outside world might think of *kimchi* as Korea's national dish, although in reality it is only a side dish. You will, however, get a small bowl with every local meal. This array of fermented vegetables comes in many forms, with spicy lettuce leaves and radish cubes as the most common.

9 Hoddeok

For dessert, try to track down some *hoddeok* – small, rice-paste pancakes filled with brown sugar and ground nuts, then fried. In warmer months these treats can be tricky to find, though a few places on Insadonggil serve them year-round.

Gimbap, **or rice rolls**

10 Gimbap

Often referred to by Westerners as "California Rolls," *gimbap* are cylindrical rolls of rice *(bap)* wrapped in layered seaweed *(gim)*. Fillings always include egg and radish, with beef, salad, and tuna among the optional extras – you'll find them on sale at cheap chain eateries such as Gimbap Cheonguk and Gimbap Nara, found all over the city.

TOP 10 KOREAN STAPLE MEALS

Mandu **dumplings**

1 Yokhoe
Pronounced "yook-hey", this dish is made with raw, minced beef and topped with slices of Korean pear, sesame seeds, and a raw egg.

2 Ojingeo Deop-bap
Chili-smothered squid *(ojingeo)* on rice *(bap)* – a zingy little dish for those who like Korean spice.

3 Bulgogi Deop-bap
Marinated beef on rice, this is one of the few Korean dishes that involves no red pepper paste whatsoever.

4 Doenjang Jjigae
A spicy soybean broth filled with goodies such as shellfish, strips of squid, and blocks of tofu.

5 Donggaseu
Pronounced "donk ass," this fried slice of breaded pork is smothered in a sweet sauce.

6 Bokkeumbap
Literally "fried rice," *Bokkeumbap* is most commonly served as a simple combination of seasoned rice, flecks of meat, and a fried egg.

7 Mandu
These are dumplings, mostly steamed. *Gogi mandu* (filled with ground beef) and *kimchi mandu* are most common.

8 Mandu Guk
In this dish, the *mandu* come in a peppery, clear soup.

9 Ddeokbokki
Delicious rice-cake chunks *(ddeok)* in a thick, and very spicy, red-pepper soup.

10 Ramyeon
Noodles served in a spicy soup with greens and an egg. Try the *chijeu ramyeon*, with a slice of processed cheese.

🔟 Restaurants

Dining at a simple food stall in Gwangjang Market

1 Gwangjang Market
광장 시장

Most of the dishes in this zany market are on view, whether pre-cooked, part-cooked, awaiting the frying pan or meant to be served raw. Popular items include *bindaeddeok* – mung-bean pancakes – and *sannakji* – baby octopus tentacles *(see p22)*.

2 OKitchen
오키친

MAP L3 ■ 50 Jongno 1-gil ■ 722 6420 ■ WWW

The Italian-flavored menu at this subterranean restaurant is the

Relaxed elegance at OKitchen

brainchild of esteemed Okinawan chef Susumu Yonaguni, who grows many of the ingredients himself on farmland outside Seoul. The desserts are uniformly superb.

3 Balwoo Gongyang
발우공양

In any other developed country, the exquisitely prepared food at Balwoo Gongyang would cost a small fortune. This restaurant is operated by monks from Jogyesa, Seoul's main Buddhist temple *(see p16)*. The set meals are highly recommended, and guests are guaranteed to be pleasantly surprised by the well-presented and delicious vegetarian cuisine served here *(see p17)*.

4 Tosokchon
토속촌

MAP K2 ■ 85-1 Chebudong ■ 737 7444 ■ WW

A popular weekend target for Seoulites, this is simultaneously the best and most attractive place in the city for *samgyetang*, a healthy soup containing a whole young chicken stuffed with ginseng, jujube, garlic, and rice.

Ichii Sushi
이찌이 스시

A small but tasty sushi place tucked away just a few minutes' walk from Gyeongbokgung. Cheerful sushi chefs welcome guests upon arrival and are happy to explain the menu. Their *tamagoyaki* (Japanese egg omlette) is excellent and the reasonably priced lunch menu includes sushi ryu and sushi jjun.

Three Pans
쓰리팬스
MAP M4■ 12-2 Gwanchuldong
■ 733 3733 ■ W

Three Pans serves different types of pork barbecue in an all-you-can-eat extravaganza. Guests get two hours to eat as much rice, meat, and kimchi they can. Children under the age of seven only have to pay 5,000 Won.

Doore
두레

Housed in a *hanok* abode built in the early 1900s, Doore serves delicious imitations of imperial-court cuisine. The interiors are decorated with scrolls and paintings, and the meals are served in beautiful handmade bowls and trays. The set meal here is a good option, though there's also an à la carte menu which features intriguing takes on the humble *bibimbap* (see p73).

Jaha Sonmandoo
자하 손만두

This is the most popular restaurant in the Buamdong area and rightly so. This spot specializes in dumplings,

not the factory-filled sort you often get in Korea, but sumptuous, handmade, beautifully presented rounds filled with all sorts of fresh and delicious goodies (see p73).

Jeon Daegamdaek
전대감댁

A little hard to find and with no English signage, this excellent spot is well worth seeking out, with delectable Korean dishes such as *jeon* (savory pancakes) and kimchi-tofu, washed down with a select choice of *makgeolli* rice beer. Head to the courtyard area out back for the best atmosphere (see p73).

Stylish Woo Lae Oak

Woo Lae Oak
우래옥

One of Seoul's oldest restaurants, Woo Lae Oak was started by North Koreans in 1945, just before the outbreak of the Korean War. Now housed in a retro building, it's revered as the best place in South Korea to try North Korea's signature dish, *naengmyeon* – a bowl of cold buckwheat noodles served in a spicy soup (*mul naengmyeon*) or an even spicier paste (*bibim naengmyeon*), and topped with a boiled egg and Korean pear (see p81).

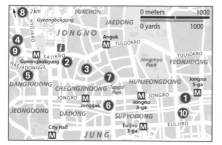

Tearooms

A large selection of teas at O'sulloc

1 O'sulloc
오설록

MAP M3 ■ 170 Gwanhundong ■ 732 6437 ■ Open 9am–10pm daily

Korea's largest tea company, O'sulloc has a few tearooms in Seoul. Try the green teas: besides over a dozen grades of the regular brew, they offer green-tea latte, tiramisu, biscuits, and other delectable goodies.

2 Mongmyeok Sanbang
몽멱 산방

MAP D3 ■ Namsan ■ 318 4790

The tearooms in and around Insadong are charming enough, but this place has licked for location – it is part way up Namsan, Seoul's mini-mountain, and sur-rounded by maple and pine trees.

3 Cha Masineun Tteul
차마시는뜰

MAP L2 ■ 35–169 Samcheongdong ■ 722 7006 ■ Open 10am–10pm daily

Tucked into the side-streets of Bukchon Hanok Village *(see pp32–3)*, this structure dates from the early 1900s. They have a wide range of teas, and some tables offer wonderful views.

4 Dalsae Neun Dal Man Saenggak Handa

달새는 달만 생각한다

MAP M3 ■ 60 Gwanhundong ■ 720 6229 ■ Open 10am–11pm daily

With a fanciful name meaning "Moon Birds Think Only of the Moon," this tearoom offers wonderful traditional brews in a secluded, faux-rustic setting.

5 Suyoil
수요일

MAP M3 ■ 23 Gwanhundong ■ 723 0191 ■ Open 9am–11pm daily

One of the older tearooms on Insadonggil, Insadong's main street, Suyoil boasts high ceilings and giant windows, but manages to retain a modern feel. It is quite popular with young couples.

6 Suyeon Sanbang
수연산방

MAP D1 ■ 248 Seongbukdong ■ 764 1736 ■ Open 11:30am–10pm daily

Most of the *hanok* tearooms in Insadong are re-creations of traditional abodes, but this is the real deal. A well-preserved wooden house, it was once the home of Sangheo, a noted local author, in the early 1940s. A dreamy place, whether you're sitting inside or out in the garden.

Traditional seating, Suyeon Sanbang

7 Dawon
다원

MAP M3 ■ 30–1 Gwanhundong ■ 730 6305 ■ Open 10:30am–10:30pm daily

In good weather it's hard to choose between Dawon's outdoor tables and those in the beautiful rooms. If you choose the latter, you'll be sitting, in traditional fashion, on floor mats. It is part of the Kyungin art complex.

8 Gahwadang
가화당

MAP D2 ■ 35–103 Samcheongdong ■ 738 2460 ■ Open 1–8pm Tue–Sun

A tiny, traditional tearoom housed in a *hanok* building almost as old as the country itself – with classic roof tiles and earthenware pots. Unlike most tearooms in the area, the focus here is firmly on green tea.

Beautiful Tea Museum

9 Beautiful Tea Museum
아름다운 차 박물관

MAP A6 ■ 193–1 Insadong ■ 735 6678 ■ Open 10:30am–10pm daily

Part museum, part shop, part school, and part tearoom, this is housed in a *hanok*-style building, though in good weather visitors may make use of the charming courtyard.

10 Margot
마고

MAP N1 ■ 129–5 Wonseodong ■ 747 3152 ■ Open 11am–7pm Tue–Sun

An elegant tearoom with a traditional appearance, serving wonderful teas, all made from organic ingredients.

TOP 10 KOREAN TEAS

Omija-cha, made with berries

1 Nok-cha
Green tea, which is available in many different grades – although it can be quite hard to tell the difference unless you're a connoisseur.

2 Saenggang-cha
A highly popular wintertime drink, ginger tea is excellent if you can feel a cough or a cold coming on.

3 Daechu-cha
Another winter warmer, this time made from the *daechu* – a kind of date also known as a *jujube*.

4 Yuja-cha
A traditional herbal tea with strips of peel from the *yuzu* citrus fruit, and often sweetened with honey or sugar.

5 Omija-cha
Even better ice-cold than hot, this lurid pink brew is made from the "five-flavored" *omija* berry.

6 Maesil-cha
Many Koreans make this slightly sour plum tea at home in the spring.

7 Mogwa-cha
Made with Chinese quince, this tea is often served in winter, when it's mixed with cinnamon.

8 Bori-cha
A simple tea made from roasted barley that you might be served at cafés and restaurants, alongside your meal.

9 Insam-cha
Tea made with ginseng, and served in a range of styles. The powder is a popular tourist purchase, particularly the red ginseng variety (*hongsam*).

10 Ssanghwa-cha
A bitter, deep brown concoction made from medicinal herbs and revered for its health-giving properties.

Cafés

Stylish interior design at Café aA

① Café aA
카페 aA

In student-filled Hongdae there's almost a café on every corner. However, few are truly unique. Step into Café aA, one of the most intriguing and distinctive cafés in Seoul. The focus here is on furniture – there are two museum-like floors, featuring chairs by the likes of Salvador Dalí and Jean Prouvé. Those on the café floor are also miniature works of art *(see p97)*.

② The Lounge
더라운지

This wonderful café-cum-restaurant is located in the Park Hyatt hotel *(see p114)* and features floor-to-ceiling

Panoramic windows at The Lounge

windows offering stunning views of Seoul. The smoothies, created by top Brazilian sports nutritionist Patricia Teixeira, are highly recommended *(see p102)*.

③ Sanmotoonge
산모퉁이

This is one of Seoul's most delightful places to relax with a cup of coffee. Sanmotoonge's outdoor terrace provides vistas of Bukhansan National Park to the north, and the Seoul fortress walls to its east. It's also a fair uphill walk from the nearest public transportation – a perfect opportunity to burn off some calories before you sit down for coffee and cake *(see p31)*.

④ Café Yung
카페 융

MAP P4 ■ **27-2 Palpandong**
■ **736 7652**

The best of the locally themed dessert cafés to have emerged in recent years, Café Yung serves tweaks on Korean delicacies such as *hoddeok* – a sort of small, sweet pancake made with rice and filled with brown sugar, cinnamon, and nuts. The persimmon yogurt is also rather delicious.

Previous pages Vibrant fall foliage at beautiful Nami Island

⑤ Club Espresso
클럽 에스프레소

The second floor of this café is a treasure trove of coffee beans from all over the globe. It is a popular place with expats – many of whom buy their coffee beans here. You can buy ready-made bags, or choose from dozens of varieties, many of which are ground to order *(see p75)*.

⑥ Café Madang
카페 마당

Located in the basement of the Hermès store in Apgujeong, the food in this café-cum-restaurant is pricey, but a cup of coffee is quite affordable – surprising, given the fact that your cup, the sugar spoon, and the table you're seated at will all be extremely expensive Hermès originals *(see p102)*.

Relaxed elegance at 74

⑧ 74
The coffee at 74 is top notch, and the establishment is quite superbly designed. You might want to head back for a designer martini in the evening *(see p102)*.

⑨ Doldamgil
돌담길

Don't miss the chance to drink coffee in Doldamgil *(see p83)*, in the grounds of the Deoksugung palace. Not only are the views wonderful, but you'll be recreating history – King Gojong's own caffeine addiction developed here.

⑩ Books Cooks
북스쿡스

This café in a renovated *hanok* abode is a cozy, pleasantly dim venue in the winter. In warmer months, the ceiling is retracted, turning it into an airy courtyard. Their handmade scones are scrumptious *(see p75)*

Sleek Café Madang

⑦ Han River Bridge Cafés
한강 선상카페

The Han River splits Seoul into two, but traditionally there were few restaurants or cafés that offered decent views of this wide waterway. In 2009, the city government sponsored the creation of cafés on six Han River bridges – they make great pit-stops if you're touring the south bank by bicycle.

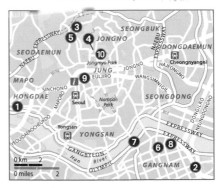

🔟 Bars

Decadent decor at Pierre's Bar

1 Pierre's Bar
피에르 바

On the 35th floor of the Lotte Hotel, this swanky bar offers stunning views of northern Seoul. The extensive wine list has personal selections by well-known French chef Pierre Gagnaire, whose restaurant sits next door. The bar also serves reasonably priced beer and cocktails (see p83).

2 Damotori
다모토리

One of the best *makgeolli (see opposite)* bars in Seoul, Damotori offers over 30 varieties of the popular alcoholic drink. If you are trying *makgeolli* for the first time, order the sampler tray, which serves five different varieties in beautiful, handmade pieces of pottery. You will also be told the best order in which to drink them (see p90).

3 Bermuda
버뮤다

MAP Q6 ▪ 34–50 Itaewondong ▪ 749 0427

Offering over 100 different wines, delightful side dishes, and some of the freshest cocktails in all of Seoul, Bermuda is one of the city's hottest bars. It consists of three floors and a terrace. The top floor can be booked for private gatherings and parties.

4 Neurin Maeul
느린 마을

MAP M4 ▪ 67 Suhadong ▪ 6030 0999

This *makgeolli* brewery is taking the drink into uncharted territory, having gone for the luxury angle with this splendid restaurant-bar. As well as seasonal variations of their own brews, they've an excellent selection of dishes – savory pancakes known as *jeon* go best with the rice beer.

5 Le Chamber
르 챔버

A secretive bar with a hidden entrance, to get in you'll need to take out a certain book on the bookshelf-cum-door. The dark interior and suited-up bartenders are reminiscent of speakeasy bars from the American Prohibition era (see p105).

6 Craftworks Taphouse
크래프트웍스 탭하우스

Microbrewed beers have gained popularity in Seoul, and this bar has a decent variety on offer. All beers are named after Korean mountain ranges – try the Geumgang Dark Ale, the Namsan Pilsner, the Seorak Oatmeal Stout, or the Jirisan Moon Bear IPA (see p90).

Craftworks Taphouse

7 Dduk Tak
뚝딱

The emphasis of this Hongdae establishment is on different takes on rice wine, rather than the drink itself. Mixes made with fruit juice are the most popular – banana, kiwi, and strawberry are all highly recommended *(see p96)*.

8 Baekseju Maeul
백세주마을

This restaurant-bar focuses on traditional Korean drinks, with Baekseju being its specialty. Other drinks are also available, including the rare *ihwaju* – a deliciously gloopy *makgeolli*-like drink. Note that it is essential to order at least a little food here. Luckily, the *anju* (bar snacks) served are quite delectable. Give the *gamja jeon* (potato pancakes) a try *(see p83)*.

Baekseju Maeul

9 Club Evans
클럽 에반스

One of the best jazz bars in the country, Club Evans is located in Hongdae, which is mainly popular with students. It plays host to a couple of sets each night – stay for both and relax over a drink in between *(see p96)*.

10 Magpie
맥파이

Initially the hobby project of an ale-loving expat, this bar continues to grow in both popularity and size. The brews here are as good as you'll find in Seoul, and the pizzas, all made to order, make for a tasty bar snack *(see p90)*.

TOP 10 KOREAN ALCOHOLIC DRINKS

Makgeolli **in traditional kettles**

1 Makgeolli
A milky-colored, still-fermenting rice wine, *makgeolli* has become hugely popular among young Koreans.

2 Baekseju
This nutty, wine-strength brew is made with ginseng, cinnamon, ginger, and other healthy ingredients. Try it in draft form at Baekseju Maeul *(see p83)*.

3 Bokbunjaju
Convenience stores sell this sweet wine in factory-made form, but the real deal can be bought near Bukhansan National Park *(see pp28–9)* during fall.

4 Maehwasu
This sugary *baekseju*-like traditional drink is made with the flower of the *maesil* – a kind of Korean green plum.

5 Dongdongju
Very similar to *makgeolli*, *dongdongju* is sold by the bowl in most restaurants selling Korean pancakes known as *jeon*.

6 Maesilju
Like *maehwasu*, this tart, sugary drink is made with *maesil* plums.

7 Yakju
Yakju means "medicinal alcohol." One popular variety is Dandelion Daepo, flavored with the flower.

8 Soju
The official national drink, *soju* is traditionally made with sweet potato.

9 Wine
Majuang is the main local brand, or try Jinro House Wine, an almost pop-like drink made with grape juice and *soju*.

10 Beer
The main brands – OB, Cass, and Hite – are cheap and available everywhere, often in draft form.

🔟 Shops and Markets

Yido Pottery, with its wide selection of ceramics

 Yido Pottery
이도 도자기

Korea was once famed across Asia for its pottery. A trawl around this multilevel shop (see p74) makes it evident why its popularity remains. Yido features complete ranges from a number of artisans, most of whom learned their trade at Hongdae.

2 Gwangjang Market
광장시장

There is fantastic food to be had at Gwangjang Market, and though that's the major draw, there is also a range of shopping on offer. The fabrics are excellent – many top Korean designers source their material here – and there's a good selection of second-hand clothing on the second level of the market (see p22).

 Yongsan Electronics Market
용산전자상가
MAP C4 ■ Hangangno 2-ga

South Korea is justly renowned for its electronic goods, with the likes of Samsung, LG, and Daewoo all big players in the international market. The market areas stretching from Yongsan station specialize in electronic goods – to find the real bargains, take the pedestrian walkway across the train tracks.

 Bespoke Tailoring

Tailored clothing is excellent value in Seoul, with the Itaewon district particularly recommended for shirts and suits. The main road, Itaewonno, has many shops. Tell your tailor if your visit is a brief one; most will try to suit your schedule.

5 Galleria
갤러리아

If you're looking for designer clothing, head to Apgujeong's twin

Galleria's twin malls

Galleria malls. The eastern wing is more luxurious, while the western wing has more Korean designers – and is a work of art in itself, paneled with scales of plastic that light up quite spectacularly at night *(see p104)*.

6 Boon the Shop
분더샵

This prestigious shop sells wares from most of Korea's top designers, as well as a selection from overseas. Local menswear labels, meanwhile, can be found at a sister mall just down the road *(see p104)*.

7 Dongdaemun Market
동대문시장

The Dongdaemun area's many malls are Seoul's greatest shopping draws. Many visitors from Japan and other Asian nations weekend in South Korea for this purpose alone, and, given the incredible range of clothing on offer, it's easy to see why. The huge Doosan Tower is the largest of the malls, though Migliore and Hello apM aren't far behind *(see p22)*.

8 Furniture
MAP M3 ▪ Tongin: 16 Gwanhundong ▪ 733 4867

South Korea produces some wonderful, Oriental-style furniture, and some places sell genuine antiques from Joseon times: Tongin in Insadong is highly recommended. Far cheaper, however, are modern re-creations of dynastic-era styles. You'll find shops full of such items along the road north of Itaewon station.

9 Ssamziegil
쌈지길

This spiraling, modern market complex is one of the best places to buy souvenirs. There are dozens of outlets, and you'll find everything from bamboo earrings to fans made

Souvenirs for sale at Ssamziegil

with mulberry paper. Given the market's popularity with tourists, prices are surprisingly fair *(see p17)*.

10 Maison de Lee Young Hee
이영희 한복집

Few foreigners venture into the world of *hanbok*, Korea's traditional clothing. Though beautiful, the outfits are expensive and far too cumbersome for regular use. Lee Young Hee is the most famed of the few local designers to have incorporated *hanbok* styles into regular clothing, even counting Hillary Clinton as a customer at her New York City outlet *(see p104)*.

Seoul for Free

Changing of the guard ceremony

1 Changing of the Guard, Gyeongbokgung

10am, 1pm & 3pm daily (except Wed)
Tickets for Seoul's grandest palace (see pp12–13) can be bought very cheaply, but you don't have to pay a single won to see the spectacular changing of the guard ceremony, which takes place in and around the front courtyard. Dozens of guards parade in flowing silken robes, backed by the palace buildings and the mountains beyond – it is about as photogenic as Seoul gets.

2 Bukchon Traditional Culture Center

MAP M1 ■ Gyedong 105 ■ 9am–6pm Mon–Fri, 10am–5pm Sat & Sun ■ bukchon.seoul.go.kr
This small cultural center is located in a renovated *hanok* – wooden houses that the entire Korean population once resided in, which are now uncomfortably close to extinction. Knot-making, calligraphy, and tea ceremonies are among the workshops and classes hosted here, and many of them are free.

3 Bukchon Hanok Ilgil

For the classic tradition-meets-modernity shot, head up to the top of this charming, slightly hard-to-find street in the Bukchon neighborhood (see pp32–3). The tiled rooftops of wooden *hanok* houses fish-scale their way down the hill, backed by the bulky skyscrapers of Seoul's main business district.

4 Namsan

You can pay to take a cable car up this small mountain (see pp24–5), rising from the center of Seoul, and you can pay to ascend the television tower at its summit. However, it's easy enough to walk up for free, and the views from the top are already spectacular enough for most visitors.

5 Hangang Paths

The wide Hangang River flows through Seoul from east to west, and it is lined on both sides, for almost the entirety of its journey through the city, by pleasant walking and cycling paths. This is where to come to see some true Seoul life: couples sharing rice beer on the riverbank, octo-genarians maintaining their health on free exercise equipment, and groups of friends eating meat from tiny barbecue sets.

6 Art Galleries

There are more than 100 art galleries in the tight area between Samcheongdong and Insadong, and most of them are free to visit. You could spend a whole day admiring art – mostly local – along this easily walkable stretch, with top targets including the Kukje (see p14), Hyundai (see pp14–15), and Insa Art Center galleries (see p16).

The Kukje, a free art gallery in Seoul

7 National Museum of Korea

This museum will get you up to speed with the history of Korea (including the now-separate North), with a wealth of artifacts from every major historical period. The golden jewelry from the Baekje and Silla periods is especially notable *(see pp20–21)*.

8 Cheonggyecheon

Seoul isn't the world's most pedestrian-friendly city, but you can walk uninterrupted for more than 5 miles (8 km) along the banks of this enchanting, below-street-level stream *(see p22)*, which reaches all the way east to the Hangang River.

Cheonggyecheon river

9 Samsung d'light

The largest of Korea's giant conglomerates, Samsung doesn't just make phones – skyscrapers, ships, and theme parks are also pumped out by this "family" business. However, its electronics arm is by far the most interesting, and you can get a sneak peek of what they have planned for the future in a showroom in the basement of the company headquarters *(see p100)*.

10 Gwangjang Market

Markets often start to look – and smell – alike, but Gwangjang *(see p23)* is quintessential Seoul, even if you're not buying anything. Stroll through in the evening, to see steam rising from all manner of boiling and frying food, garrulous businessmen with rice beer-reddened cheeks, and the occasional character turning up with an accordion or trumpet.

TOP 10 BUDGET TIPS

Buskers in a university area

1 Transport Cards
Pre-paid travel cards *(see p109)* will save you money on the bus and subway, and they can also be used for taxi journeys.

2 Convenience Stores
Seoul has no shortage of cheap convenience stores such as 7-Eleven, CU, and GS25 – all of them open around the clock.

3 Performance Tickets
Save up to 70 percent by booking at the Korea Tourism Organization head office, near Cheonggyecheon *(see p113)*.

4 Tax Refunds
You can get 10 percent back on certain goods when leaving Korea.

5 Drinking Water
Free water fountains can be found all over the city – including many hotel rooms.

6 Stick to the North
Restaurants and cafés are usually more expensive south of the river.

7 Korea Grand Sale
Most city shops participate in discounts and special offers in this huge sale in January and February.

8 Gimbap Cheonguk
This is a restaurant chain whose ubiquitous outlets serve cheap, tasty Korean staples.

9 University Areas
You'll find the cheapest restaurants, bars, and fashion stores in western Seoul, around its many universities.

10 Tipping
Tips are almost unheard of in Korea – you pay what you're asked for.

Festivals and Events

Bongeunsa temple decorated for the Lotus Lantern Festival

1 Seoul International Women's Film Festival

Mid-Apr ■ www.siwff.or.kr

This film festival, held each year in Seoul, screens movies, documentaries, and short works by famous and independent women filmmakers from across the globe.

2 Cherry Blossom Season
Usually Apr

Spring heralds the cherry blossom season, with gorgeous blossoms weighing down the city's many cherry trees. Yeouido's riverfront is the standard viewing area for Seoulites, though those in the know make a beeline for the less crowded Seoul Grand Park (see p34).

Cherry blossom in Yeouido

3 Lotus Lantern Festival
May

On Buddha's birthday Seoul's various temples decorated with thousands of colorful lanterns – a sight just as spectacular by night as it is by day. Jogyesa temple (see p16) is the hub of proceedings, though the mountains of Bukhansan National Park (see pp28–9), which is home to several temples, offer a more relaxing experience.

4 Jongmyo Daejae
1st Sun in May

The kings of the Joseon dynasty (1392–1910) venerated their ancestors five times a year at the Jongmyo shrines (see p27). Though Korean royalty has long faded into history, the spectacular ceremony is re-enacted each spring, and it is one of the most traditional and beautiful events in Seoul's calendar.

5 Jisan Valley and Pentaport Rock Festivals

Late Jul ■ Jisan Valley: www.valley rockfestival.mnet.com ■ Pentaport: www.pentaportrock.com

Seoul's two main rock festivals take place simultaneously at separate venues just outside the city. Japan's Fuji Rock takes place at almost the same time, bringing quite a few big international groups to the area.

6 Seoul Plaza Events
MAP L5 ■ Throughout summer

Free musical performances, many traditionally Korean in nature, take place each summer evening on Seoul Plaza.

7 Seoul Open Night
Aug

This is a night of performances throughout the city, with free shuttle buses ferrying revelers between venues. Some Seoul sights, including some palaces, stay open until midnight – an annual opportunity to see them under cover of nighttime.

8 Seoul Drum Festival
■ www.seouldrum.go.kr (Check website for schedule)

A mix of international and local ensembles play at this event that encourages audience participation. Even if you're not hauled onstage to embarrass yourself in front of a crowd, you'll be able to take lessons in playing traditional Korean drums.

Seoul's Fireworks Festival

9 Fireworks Festival
Early Oct ■ www. hanwhafireworks.com

The most explosive event of the year takes place on Yeouido's riverfront. It is hugely popular, so arrive early to ensure viewing space.

10 Seoul Performing Arts Festival
Oct ■ www.spaf.or.kr

Seoul has fantastic performances throughout the year, but SPAF is a particular highlight, showcasing an eclectic range of troupes. Venues are spread around the Daehangno area.

TOP 10 HOLIDAYS

Drummers on Liberation Day

1 Jan 1, New Year's Day
New Year's Day sees Seoulites partying, with City Hall as the focal point.

2 Mar 1, Independence Day
With flags galore, South Korea commemorates the 1919 movement against Japanese annexation. A reading of the Declaration of Independence takes place in Tapgol Park.

3 Mar 14, White Day
Though not a national holiday, White Day sees girls buying gifts for their men, a month after Valentine's Day.

4 Apr/May, Buddha's Birthday
Seoul's temples and streets are strewn with lanterns celebrating Buddha's birthday.

5 May 5, Children's Day
Parents take their children to amusement parks or zoos for a day of fun and games.

6 Jun 6, Memorial Day
A commemoration of those who died in service or in the independence movement.

7 Aug 15, Liberation Day
The day of the Allied victory over Japan, which resulted in Korea's independence.

8 Oct 3, National Foundation Day
Celebrates the founding of the first Korean state in 2333 BC by the legendary god-king Dangun.

9 Nov 11, Pepero Day
This is not a national holiday, but on this day convenience stores are crammed with Koreans buying their loved ones Pepero chocolate sticks.

10 Dec 25, Christmas Day
Christmas is observed as a national holiday in Korea.

Excursions from Seoul

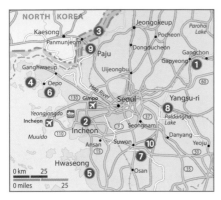

③ The DMZ
비무장 지대

MAP F1 ■ www.korea
dmztour.com

The Demilitarized Zone (DMZ) dividing North and South Korea may be one of the more dangerous borders on earth, but it is one of the most popular excursions for visitors to Seoul. Tours of the zone, which include the Joint Security Area (JSA), also offer the chance to step a few meters across the border under the eye of watchful – and armed – guards.

① Nami Island
남이섬

MAP G1 ■ Namiseom ■ 753 1247 ■ www.namisum.com

This small, tree-filled island found fame in the early noughties as a filming location in *Winter Sonata*, a local drama series. The initial hordes of drama buffs have subsided, and the island's pristine pathways are now perfect for a quiet stroll.

Colorful foliage at Nami Island

② Incheon
인천

MAP F2

Though most visitors to Korea arrive in Incheon, few see anything of the city itself – a pity, as its sights can easily fill half a day. Visit the gentrified Chinatown for a bowl of *jjajangmyeon* – noodles in black-bean sauce – before strolling up to Jayu Park for a view over the sea.

④ Seongmodo
석모도

MAP F1

Of the hundreds of Korean islands that jut up from the Yellow Sea (known locally as the "West Sea"), Seongmodo is the most accessible from Seoul. The Buddhist temple of Bomunsa is the island's most vaunted sight, though some prefer to rent a bicycle and take off on the country roads.

⑤ Hwaseong
화성

MAP F2

This stunning fortress was built in the 1790s on the orders of King Yeongjo *(see p39)*, and intended to be the hub of a new Korean capital. Now a UNESCO-listed site, the fortress walls make for a superb walk, affording views of Suwon, the modern city that sprung up around it.

⑥ Ganghwado
강화도

MAP F1

Located to the west of Seoul, this island was the main point of attack for most of the foreign powers who have attempted an invasion of Korea. Its attractions include UNESCO-listed dolmen, and you can feast on fresh seafood in the port of Oepo.

7 Korean Folk Village
한국 민속촌
MAP G2 ■ 107 Boradong, Yongin City
■ 031 288 0000 ■ Adm
■ www.koreanfolk.co.kr

This re-creation of a Joseon-dynasty village offers a peek into the Korea of yesteryear. Dirt tracks weave between wooden houses, and performances take place throughout the day. While the "farmers' dance" is the undoubted highlight, look out for the Joseon wedding and the tightrope show too.

8 Yangsu-ri
양수리
MAP G1

Almost at the eastern periphery of the gargantuan Seoul subway network, and surrounded by pine-clad mountains, this village lies at the confluence of two rivers, which merge to form Seoul's Hangang. The action is centered on a picturesque island, where walking trails weave between rice fields to highly photogenic viewpoints *(see p60)*.

9 Paju Book City
파주 책마을
MAP F1

Most of Seoul's book publishers are based in this well-designed modern area west of the capital, full of

Forest of Wisdom Library, Paju

appealing architecture. It makes for pleasant walking territory, and there are some great cafés and libraries, often within the quarters of the publishers themselves.

10 Everland
에버랜드
MAP G2

You would do well to find a Korean who hasn't been to this theme-park south of Seoul – more than 7 million come here every year to enjoy the zoo, golf course, rides, and other attractions, including a surprisingly good museum full of Buddhist art.

Garden Terrace and Main Stage at Everland theme park

Seoul
Area by Area

Nighttime view of downtown Seoul, with Namsan in the background

TOP10 The Palace Quarter

The area around Seoul's two oldest palaces – Gyeongbokgung and Changdeokgung – offers a glimpse into South Korea's rich history. The palaces were built in the early 15th century, with the shrine of Jongmyo erected shortly afterwards. The Palace Quarter was at the helm of independence movements – the Seodaemun Prison is a relic of the Japanese annexation of 1910–45. After independence, Korea's first president moved into the Blue House behind Gyeongbokgung. Wooden buildings from those formative decades can be seen in Insadong and Bukchon Hanok Village – areas filled with shops, art galleries, and restaurants.

Banner, Gyeongbokgung

AREA MAP OF THE PALACE QUARTER

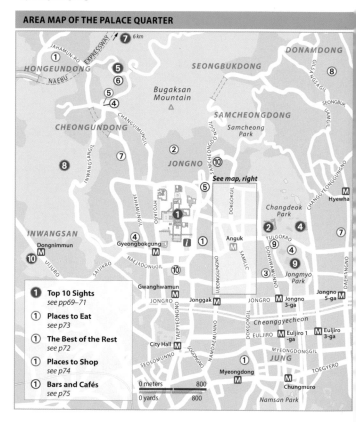

See map, right

1 **Top 10 Sights**
see pp69–71

1 **Places to Eat**
see p73

1 **The Best of the Rest**
see p72

1 **Places to Shop**
see p74

1 **Bars and Cafés**
see p75

0 meters 800
0 yards 800

The palace of Gyeongbokgung, restored after its turbulent history

1 Gyeongbokgung 경복궁
This splendid palace was built just after King Taejo (see p39) chose Seoul as the capital of his kingdom in 1392. History has not been kind to the palace – it was ravaged by fire twice in the 16th century and left in ruins for almost 300 years. Shortly after its restoration in 1888, Empress Myeongseong was assassinated here by Japanese agents. Japan formally annexed Seoul in 1910 and most of the buildings in the palace were destroyed once more. Carefully reconstructed, it is now perhaps South Korea's most popular tourist sight (see pp12–13).

2 Changdeokgung 창덕궁
A decade younger than Gyeongbokgung, and with a similar history, Changdeokgung is much better preserved – one reason behind its inclusion on UNESCO's World Heritage list. Some artifacts here date back to the 1410s, most notably a small bridge named Geumcheongyo. At the back of the palace lie verdant grounds, with paths winding towards the revered "Secret Garden," which has a beautiful lake at its center (see pp26–7).

Ceiling detail, Changdeokgung

3 Bukchon Hanok Village
북촌 한옥 마을

Traditional Korean houses – wooden affairs known as *hanok* – are a rarity in modern Seoul. The Bukchon area, however, retains clutches of such abodes, arrayed along winding side-streets. Wander along these delight-ful streets and, whichever way you go, you are sure to stumble across a quaint tearoom, a tiny gallery, or one of the many museums in the area *(see pp32–3)*.

Bukchon Hanok Village

4 Changgyeonggung 창경궁
The third major palace in the area, Changgyeonggung, though not as popular as the others, is said by some to be the most picturesque. Witness to a royal murder in 1762 *(see p38)*, it is a surviving relic of the Japanese Empire's transformation of the palace into Korea's first theme park *(see pp26–7)*.

5 Buamdong 부암동
Situated to the north of Gyeongbokgung palace, Buamdong, though relatively underdeveloped, has become extremely popular with young locals, who frequent the area's trendy cafés and restaurants. It also has two excellent galleries – Gana Art Gallery *(see p31)* and the Whanki Gallery *(see p30)*. Visitors with valid

RESILIENT SEOUL

King Taejo made Seoul the capital of the fledgling Joseon dynasty in 1394. Given what the area has been through since then – the devastation by fire of two main palaces in the 1590s; the occupation of Korea by the Japanese (1910–45); and finally, the Korean War – it is astonishing that the original structures have remained in place.

identification can now hike through Bugaksan, a mountain off-limits until 2006, and still subject to high-security surveillance *(see pp30–31)*.

6 Insadong 인사동
A popular tourist area, Insadong is markedly traditional by the standards of this resolutely modern city. Tiny side-streets meander off the main street, Insadonggil, and they feature a truly bewildering number of shops, tearooms, and galleries, most of which sell or display distinctive local fare. Sights around this area include Seoul's major Buddhist temple, Jogyesa, and the city's unofficial sixth palace, Unhyeongung *(see pp16–17)*.

7 Bukhansan National Park 북한산 국립 공원
Few world capitals can boast a national park in their catchment area, but Seoul is an exception. A popular spot, the park draws close to eight million visitors a year. Though Central Seoul is just a few miles down the road, city life feels far away when walking on one of the trails in the park. The choice of activities is wide – visit one of over a dozen temples, go rock climbing, or head to the granite peaks for a hike *(see pp28–9)*.

Trail in Bukhansan National Park

(8) Inwangsan 인왕산
MAP C1

Despite being suppressed during the reign of the Joseon dynasty (1392–1910), shamanism remains part of Korean life to this day. Local shamanists consider the mountain of Inwangsan sacred, and it is here that you are most likely to see one of the spectacular practices pertaining to the creed. Religious fervor aside, the mountain's various paths, dotted with shamanic temples and shrines, are truly beautiful.

(9) Jongmyo 종묘

Built during the rule of King Taejo, this Confucian shrine *(see p27)* has always been used for the purpose of venerating Korea's royal ancestors – there were 27 kings in the Joseon dynasty alone and, following the Confucian code, each paid respects to his predecessors five times a year. Each May sees the Jongmyo Daejae, a colorful re-enactment of the ancient ceremonies *(see p62)*.

Jongmyo shrine

(10) Seodaemun Prison History Hall
서대문 형무소역사관
MAP C2 ■ 120–80 Hyeongeodong ■ Open Mar–Oct: 9:30am–6pm, Nov–Feb: 9:30am–5pm; closed Mon ■ Adm

Seoul's most notorious prison during Japan's occupation (1910–45), this is now a museum highlighting the atrocities committed here during that time. However, it remains tight-lipped on the fact that similar acts are said to have been inflicted upon protesters well after independence. Here, it is easy to forget that South Korea was a dictatorship until the 1980s.

A DAY IN THE PALACE QUARTER

> Bukchon Hanok Village
> Gyeongbokgung
> Changgyeonggung
> Insadong   O'sulloc
> Changdeokgung
> Jogyesa   Ssamziegil
> Insa Art Center
> Sun Gallery

▶ MORNING

Begin your day with a cup of traditional Korean tea in one of Insadong's many excellent tearooms, or go for something more snazzy, like a green tea latte in **O'sulloc** *(see p50)*. From here you can take your pick of the area's three palaces – **Gyeongbokgung** *(see pp12–13)*, **Changdeokgung**, and **Changgyeonggung** *(see pp26–7)*. All are superb sights, though there's no real need to see all three. Spend the latter part of the morning getting pleasantly lost among the charming wooden abodes of **Bukchon Hanok Village** *(see pp32–3)*, before stopping for coffee in trendy Samcheongdonggil.

AFTERNOON

Head back to Insadong for lunch – almost any of the area's restaurants are worth a visit. After lunch, take a leisurely walk around the area and browse any of its galleries or shops – the **Ssamziegil** complex *(see p17)* has dozens of stores selling souvenirs, while the **Sun Gallery** *(see p72)* and **Insa Art Center** *(see p16)* are the most vaunted repositories of art. If you have both time and energy left, head to **Jogyesa** temple *(see p16)* to experience Korean Buddhism in action. Insadong is, again, best for dinner, and for a nighttime stroll. The front courtyard of Gyeongbokgung is, however, the prime sunset spot, with the mountains behind the palace catching the last beams of the day rather beautifully.

See map on pp68–9 ➤

The Best of the Rest

Gilsangsa temple

1 Gilsangsa
MAP D1 ▪ 323 Seongbukdong ▪ 3672 5945

Though a little difficult to find, this temple is less crowded and more beautiful than the more famous Jogyesa complex (see p16).

2 Cheong Wa Dae
MAP C1 ▪ 1 Cheongwadaero ▪ 730 5800 ▪ Tours at 10am, 11am, 2pm & 3pm Tue–Sat ▪ www.english.president.go.kr

Hour-long tours of the official presidential abode and its superb gardens are available. Book online at least three weeks in advance, and bring your passport.

3 Sun Gallery
MAP M3 ▪ 184 Insadong ▪ 734 0458 ▪ Open 10am–6pm Mon–Sat ▪ www.sungallery.co.kr

One of Insadong's most prestigious galleries, Sun Gallery focuses on the work of Korean artists born before 1960. Inspired by the Korean War and Japanese occupation, the art is quite powerful.

4 Jongmyo Park
Outside the entrance to the Jongmyo Shrine is one of Seoul's most idiosyncratic sights. On sunny days, this small expanse of concrete is filled with elderly Korean men playing Chinese chess (see p27).

5 Insa Art Center
Original, contemporary art is on display at this seven-floor gallery, Insadong's largest. The exhibitions change each week (see p16).

6 Unhyeongung
Often described as Seoul's sixth palace, Unhyeongung's charming wooden buildings are delightful to wander around in (see p17).

7 Daehangno
The main appeal of this student area is its range of small theaters. Although performances in English are rare, the shows can be quite a spectacle.

8 Seongnagwon
MAP D1

This is one of South Korea's prettiest gardens, though tricky access and irregular opening hours mean there are few visitors.

9 Jogyesa
Seoul's most famous temple is the headquarters of the Jogye order, Korea's main Buddhist sect. There's also a Buddhist museum on site (see p16).

10 Gwanghwamun Square
MAP L3

Near Gyeongbokgung's famous south gate, this plaza features statues of two Korean heroes – Admiral Yi Sun-shin, who repelled the Japanese invasions of the 1590s, and King Sejong (see p39), creator of the Korean alphabet.

Gwanghwamun Square

Places to Eat

PRICE CATEGORIES
For the equivalent of a meal for two made
up of a range of dishes, or one large dish,
with half a bottle of wine.

W under W20,000 WW W20,000–100,000
WWW over W100,000

Traditional interior of Seokparang

1 **Seokparang** 석파랑
MAP B1 ▪ 125 Hongjidong
▪ 395 2500 ▪ WWW

Located near the Buamdong area
(see pp30–31), this place offers
banquet meals.

2 **Balwoo Gongyang**
발우공양
MAP N3 ▪ 733 2081 ▪ WW

Vegetarian Buddhist food in a
gorgeous restaurant overlooking
Joqyesa temple. Reservations are
essential *(see p17)*.

3 **Galbi Golmok** 갈비 골목
MAP N3 ▪ 164 Myodong ▪ W

A side-street with several eateries
serving barbecued meat. As is usual
with such places in Korea, you'll
cook your own meal at the table.

4 **Jeon Daegamdaek**
전대감댁
MAP M2 ▪ 194 Chaebudong
▪ 070 4202 5170 ▪ WWW

If the weather allows it, grab a
courtyard seat at this tiny restaurant
serving tasty Korean fare *(see p47)*.

5 **Jaha Sonmandoo**
자하 손만두
MAP C1 ▪ 245–2 Buamdong
▪ 379 2648 ▪ W

Try dumplings with fillings such as
shiitake mushrooms and leek here.

6 **Doore** 두레
MAP C2 ▪ 8–7 Insadong
▪ 732 2919 ▪ WW

This restaurant, located on a tiny
side-street, offers traditional dishes
with a contemporary edge.

7 **Jihwaja** 지화자
MAP C1 ▪ 125 Jahamun-ro
▪ 2269 5834 ▪ WW

Jihwaja is a Korean restaurant that
specializes in royal cuisine – dishes
once served to the royal family.

8 **Pureun Byeol** 푸른별
MAP M3 ▪ 118–15
Gwanhundong ▪ 734 3095 ▪ W

A popular place serving dishes from
the mountains of Gangwon province.
Try the *deodeok* (bellflower root).

Elegant cuisine at Nwijo

9 **Nwijo** 뉘조
MAP M3 ▪ 84–13
Gwanhundong ▪ 730 9311 ▪ WW

In a beautiful *hanok* building, this
restaurant serves a mix of Buddhist
temple food and court cuisine.

10 **Dudaemunjip** 두대문집
MAP M3 ▪ 64 Gwanhundong
▪ 737 0538 ▪ W

Try Korean staples such as *bibimbap*
as well as meals like *ddeok galbi*
(seasoned meat patties) here.

See map on pp68–9

Places to Shop

1 **Ssamziegil** 쌈지길
A multilevel shopping complex, Ssamziegil has dozens of trinket shops. Almost all stores here sell distinctly Korean fare *(see p17)*.

2 **Sami** 사미
MAP M3 ▪ 182 Insadong
This tiny store sells an interesting selection of women's clothing – rustic and traditionally Buddhist in appearance, but with a contemporary edge.

3 **Lee Geon Maan** 이건만
MAP M3 ▪ 197–4 Gwanhundong ▪ 733 8265
The ties, bags, and purses created by this upscale label feature characters from the Korean alphabet Hangul as part of their design.

4 **Bizeun** 빚은
MAP M4 ▪ 37 Insadong ▪ 738 1245
A small store, Bizeun sells delicious and colorful rice cakes that make fascinating souvenirs.

5 **Kwang Ju Yo** 광주요
MAP M1 ▪ 203 Gahoedong ▪ 741 4801
A renowned pottery brand housed in a beautiful store, Kwang Ju Yo offers superbly designed tea sets, bowls, vases, and more.

Pottery display at Kwang Ju Yo

6 **Yido Pottery** 이도 도자기
MAP M1 ▪ 10–6 Gahoedong ▪ 722 0756
This large shop sells contemporary Korean pottery from top local talents. Many pieces are very affordable.

7 **Korea Culture and Design Foundation Gallery (KCDF)** 갤러리
MAP M3 ▪ 182–2 Gwanhundong ▪ 733 9041
This store sells nicer trinkets than most other shops in Insadong. It also has pottery and paper products.

8 **Sorihana** 소리하나
MAP M3 ▪ 31 Gwanhundong ▪ 738 8335
Sorihana sells a range of pendants and fans, as well as traditional silk wrappings known as *bojagi*. Also available are silk ties with the Korean alphabet woven into abstract designs.

9 **Sowyen** 소연
MAP P2 ▪ 149 Seosullagil ▪ 546 2498
The jewelry sold in Sowyen has a distinct East Asian edge. This branch also has a café.

10 **Tongin Building** 통인빌딩
MAP M3 ▪ 16 Gwanhundong ▪ 733 4867
Go hunting for antique furniture from the Joseon era on the upper floors of this Colonial building.

Bars and Cafés

1 Dugahun 두가헌
MAP L2 ■ 80 Sagandong
■ 3210 2100
Just across the road from
Gyeongbokgung palace *(see pp12–13)*, Dugahun offers one of the best
selections of wines in the city.

Dugahun wine bar

2 LN 엘엔
MAP M1 ■ 27–1 Hwadong
■ 722 3152
A re-created *hanok*, LN is a great
place to kick back over a coffee or
tea after a hectic day of sightseeing.
Note that you'll be sitting on the
floor, Korean-style.

3 Pureun Byeol 푸른별
More of a restaurant than a
bar, Pureun Byeol is a delightful
venue offering a range of home-made *makgeolli* cocktails *(see p73)*.

4 Club Espresso
클럽 에스프레소
MAP C1 ■ 237–1 Buamdong
■ 764 8719
Many expatriates head to Buamdong
for the sole purpose of visiting this
café, which offers Seoul's best range
of coffee beans. Visitors can sample
the brews before buying.

5 La Cle 라 끌레
MAP M1 ■ 95–1
Samcheongdong ■ 734 7752
In the 1980s, this basement bar was
a hangout for anti-government
protesters. It is now one of the city's
best jazz venues – performances
take place most evenings.

6 Sanmotoonge 산모퉁이
A bit of an uphill trek from the
nearest bus stop, Sanmotoonge is
well worth the effort. The terraces
offer amazing views *(see p30)*.

7 Sanchez 산체즈
MAP M2 ■ 26 Yunboseongil
■ 4202 5170
A favorite with those who love their
makgeolli rice beer. The owner also
whips up quirky fusion dishes in his
open kitchen – a pity that there are
only four tables.

8 Remini's 레미니스
MAP M2 ■ 120–1 Gyedong
■ 3675 0406
A small café-cum-bakery tucked into
the charming streets of Bukchon
Hanok Village *(see pp32–3)*. Try one
of the delectable desserts.

9 Books Cooks 북스쿡스
MAP M1 ■ 177–4 Gahoedong
■ 743 4003
This appealing café is part-traditional
Korean house and part-English
tearoom. A wide range of teas are
available here, and delicious scones
are baked to order.

Scones at
Books Cooks

**10 The Second Best
Place in Seoul**
서울에서 둘째로 잘하는 집
MAP D1 ■ 28–21 Samcheongdong
■ 734 5302
Poking fun at Korea's obsession with
superlatives, this venue is famous for
patjuk – a red-bean porridge served
with chestnuts and cinnamon.

See map on pp68–9

TOP 10 Central Seoul

Artifact, Seoul Museum of History

Seoul's central districts are supremely businesslike in nature: a near unbroken swath of glassy skyscrapers looms over the streets all the way from City Hall to Dongdaemun, with the gaps in between, and occasionally below, filled with shops. Once you delve into the area, you will find some of Seoul's best sights – two palaces from the Joseon dynasty, museums and galleries, and a re-creation of a traditional village. There's also a small but impressive range of Colonial-era buildings. Add to the mix superb restaurants and cafés, and you have a recipe for at least a few days of sightseeing.

1 Cheonggyecheon 청계천

One of Seoul's most popular walking areas with locals and visitors alike, this stream attracted a huge amount of criticism on its opening in 2005 – a little peculiar, given that it is considerably more beautiful than the elevated highway it replaced. Construction costs aside, it's a stunner – and the streamside walkways stretch all the way to the Han River (see p22).

Walkway along Cheonggyecheon

AREA MAP OF CENTRAL SEOUL

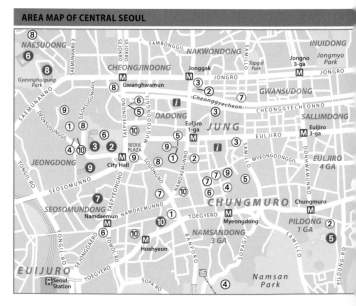

Changing of the guard at Daehanmun gate, Deoksugung palace

2 Deoksugung 덕수궁
MAP K5 ■ 5–1 Jeongdong
■ 771 9952 ■ Open 9am–9pm
Tue–Sun ■ Adm

The palace of Deoksugung was first built in 1592, after Seoul's other palaces were burned down in the Japanese invasions. Much of its recent history also relates to Japan – King Gojong fled to this palace in 1897 after the assassination of his wife, and lived here for most of the period of Japanese occupation, during which two Neo-Classical buildings were erected. One of the buildings now houses the National Museum of Contemporary Art.

3 National Museum of Contemporary Art
국립 현대 미술관
MAP K5 ■ 5–1 Jeongdong ■ 188 6000
■ Open 9am–8:30pm Tue–Sun
■ Adm for special exhibitions
■ www.mmca.go.kr

Though this superb modern-art museum is a part of the Deoksugung palace (**above**), it is incongruously located in a Neo-Classical, Western-style building built in 1909 – evidence that the Joseon dynasty was opening up in its final years of rule. The exhibitions are always of a high standard, and tend to feature the works of local artists.

4 Dongdaemun 동대문
A famous market space, this fascinating area is spread out both indoors and outdoors. It features a culture park designed by the late architect Zaha Hadid, several streets on which Cyrillic text vies for supremacy with Korean, and the ancient city gate from which the district takes its name (see pp22–3).

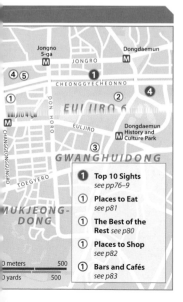

Although the buildings of Central Seoul are almost entirely modern in nature, look a little closer and you will see that the city also contains fascinating specimens from previous centuries – Dongdaemun gate and the palaces of Deoksugung and Gyeonghuigung, all of which are relics of the Joseon dynasty.

Room in Gyeonghuigung palace

5 Namsangol Hanok Village
남산골 한옥 마을
This re-created village, located on the slopes of Namsan (see pp24–5), provides a little trip back in time. Displayed here are five traditional *hanok* buildings – all dynastic-era structures pulled from other parts of the city. The buildings and their surrounding parkland make for a wonderful walk, especially in the evening, when the area glows with strings of paper lanterns (see p25).

Totem pole, Namsangol

6 Gyeonghuigung 경희궁
MAP J3 ▪ 1–126 Sinmunno 2-ga ▪ Open 9am–6pm Tue–Sun
Although not as popular as the other five palaces in Seoul, Gyeonghuigung is nevertheless a truly gorgeous structure. Although simpler in

terms of layout than the others, its paintwork is stunning, and the hill behind the palace offers great views.

7 The Plateau 플라토
MAP K6 ▪ 1F, Samsung Life Insurance Building, 150 Taepyeongno 2-ga ▪ 1577 7595 ▪ Open 10am–6pm Tue–Sun ▪ Adm ▪ www.plateau.or.kr
Small but beautifully designed, this cultural venue was formerly known as the Rodin Gallery. Sculptures from the French master still feature in its main hall, the Glass Pavilion, which is illuminated almost entirely with natural light. Apart from Rodin's work, visitors can also see other pieces by local as well as foreign contemporary artists.

8 Seoul Museum of History 서울역사박물관
MAP J4 ▪ Sinmunno 2-ga ▪ 724 0274 ▪ Open 9am–8pm Mon–Fri, 9am–7pm Sat & Sun (till 6pm Nov–Feb) ▪ Adm for special exhibitions ▪ www.museum.seoul.kr
This museum includes a series of rooms showcasing artifacts from

An electric streetcar from the 1930s at the Seoul Museum of History

Seoul through the ages, as well as a "Development" section providing a window into how this fast-changing city will look in the future. There are frequently changing temporary exhibitions, and the permanent displays from the Joseon era are also well worth a visit.

⑨ Seoul Museum of Art
서울시립미술관
MAP K5 ■ 37 Seosomundong
■ 124 8800 ■ Open 10am–8pm
Tue–Fri, 10am–7pm Sat & Sun
■ Adm for special exhibitions
■ www.seoulmoa.org

Known as SeMA for short, this large, airy museum is the go-to venue for exhibiting works of famous international masters, past and present. There are usually two major exhibitions held each year. Even the minor ones tend to be top-drawer, with the main focus generally on Asian art and sculpture.

Seoul Museum of Art

⑩ Shinsegae Department Store 신세계 백화점
MAP L6 ■ 52–50 Chungmuro 1-ga
■ 1588 1234 ■ Open 10:30am–8pm
■ www.shinsegae.com

Built in 1930, this is the oldest of Korea's many department stores, and despite the presence of new stores such as Galleria (see p56–7), it is still the most beautiful – especially when the Christmas decorations are up in December. Architecture aside, it is also a great place to shop for top Korean clothing and jewelry labels.

See map on pp76–7

A DAY IN CENTRAL SEOUL

▶ MORNING

Central Seoul has a range of interesting options for your morning drink – have an espresso at the **Coffee Bean & Tea Leaf** (see p83), or tea surrounded by friendly cats at the **Goyangi Darakbang** (see p83). Try coffee with authentic Belgian chocolate at **Leonidas** (see p83), or a red-bean latte at **Gildeulyeojigi** (see p83). **Doldamgil** (see p83) is a little café inside the palace of **Deoksugung** – once home to King Gojong, a noted coffee addict, who had a pavilion erected in which to enjoy his morning brew. Deoksugung also makes a great place to start the day's sightseeing – the **National Museum of Contemporary Art** (see p77) forms part of the complex, while the even more impressive **Seoul Museum of Art** is just outside.

AFTERNOON

Stop for lunch at **Pierre Gagnaire à Séoul** (see p81), then head to the streets of Myeongdong for an afternoon of shopping. If you are in the mood for some more sightseeing, hunt down **Shinsegae Department Store**, the **Former Russian Legation** (see p80), and other specimens of Japanese Colonial architecture located nearby. In the evening, walk down to **Cheonggyecheon** (see p76), a stream whose beautiful subterranean paths form the best possible route to **Gwangjang Market** (see p23) – surely Seoul's most fascinating place for an evening meal and a cup of local rice wine.

The Best of the Rest

1 Jungmyeonjeon 중명전
MAP K5 ■ 1–11 Jeongdong
■ Open 10am–4pm Tue–Sun

Designed by the Russian architect A.I. Sabatin, this is where King Gojong signed the Eulsa Treaty in 1905, paving the way for Japanese annexation.

2 Myeongdong 명동
MAP M6

This shopping area probably receives more visitors than Insadong. The majority come here to buy branded clothing, purses, or makeup.

3 Bosingak 보신각
MAP M4

Seoul's most important road was named after the bell that tolled in this belfry each evening, signaling the closure of the city gates and the beginning of the nighttime curfew.

4 Chongdong Theater 정동극장
MAP K5 ■ 8–11 Jeongdong

This is the home of *Miso*, Korea's longest-running musical. Even if you're not here for a performance, head to Gildeulyeojigi, the on-site café, for a red-bean latte.

5 Myeongdong Cathedral 명동
MAP N5 ■ 1 Myeongdong 2-ga ■ 774 1784

The focus of Korea's burgeoning Catholic faith, this 1892 cathedral is the oldest parish church in the land.

Myeongdong Cathedral

Namdaemun gate

6 Namdaemun 남대문
MAP C3 ■ 29 Namdaemun 4-ga

First built in 1398, Seoul's "Great South Gate" was ravaged by fire following an arson attack in 2008. Fully restored, it reopened in 2013.

7 Bank of Korea Museum 한국은행 화폐금융박물관
MAP L6 ■ 110 Namdaemunno 3-ga ■ 759 4881 ■ 10am–5pm Tue–Sun

This Japanese-designed structure houses a museum showcasing rare notes and coins from the world over.

8 Deoksugunggil 덕수궁 길
MAP K5

Deoksugunggil is one of Seoul's most charming roads. However, it was once home to the city's divorce courts, and some locals believe that couples walking here will soon break up.

9 Former Russian Legation 구러시아 공사관
MAP J4 ■ 15–1 Jeongdong

Designed by Sabatin, this is where King Gojong fled for protection after the assassination of his wife, Empress Myeongseong.

10 Seoul City Hall 서울특별시 청사
MAP L5 ■ 31 Taepyungno 1-ga

City Hall was first built by the Japanese in 1926 and housed the offices of the city's local government after liberation in 1945. It has since been converted into a library and a new City Hall has been built (see p43).

Places to Eat

PRICE CATEGORIES
For the equivalent of a meal for two made up of a range of dishes, or one large dish, with half a bottle of wine.

W under W20,000 **WW** W20,000–100,000
WWW over W100,000

1 **Woo Lae Oak** 우래옥
MAP D2 ■ 118–1 Joogyodong
■ 2265 0151 ■ **W**

Seoul's most famous restaurant for *naengmyeon* – buckwheat noodles in a cold soup *(mul naengmyun)* or sauce *(bibim naengmyun)*.

2 **The Korea House** 한국의 집
MAP F6 ■ 80–2 Pildong ■ 2266 9101 ■ **WW**

Indulge in a banquet similar to those once eaten by the Joseon royalty.

3 **Samarkand** 사마르칸트
MAP D2 ■ 120 Gwanghuidong 1-ga ■ 2277 4267 ■ **W**

This simple Uzbek restaurant is frequented by the traders from Seoul's little "Russia Town".

4 **Myeongdong Gyoja** 명동교자
MAP M6 ■ 25–2 Myeongdong
■ 776 5348 ■ **W**

Delicious dumplings at bargain prices – it's little wonder that the place is jam-packed every day at lunchtime.

5 **Gwangjang Market** 광장시장
MAP D2 ■ **W**

There are two intersecting lanes of snack stands and eateries in this popular market. Ask the locals for their favorites.

6 **Bulgogi Brothers** 불고기 브라더스
MAP M5 ■ 84 Seoul Finance Center ■ 775 7871 ■ **WW**

A great place for barbecued meat, this place is popular with locals and visitors alike.

7 **31 Sky Lounge** 31 스카이라운지
MAP M4 ■ 10–2 Gwancheoldong ■ 739 4619 ■ **W**

Once a hangout for VIPs and the military elite, this place is now charmingly retro in appearance, and the buffet spreads are both varied and delicious.

8 **Sushi Cho** 스시조
MAP L5 ■ 87 Sogongdong ■ 317 0373 ■ **WW**

This restaurant is located in the Westin Chosun hotel *(see p115)*, and the sushi served here is acclaimed even by the hotel's Japanese visitors.

Pierre Gagnaire à Séoul

9 **Pierre Gagnaire à Séoul** 피에르 가니에르 서울
MAP L5 ■ 1 Sogongdong ■ 317 7181 ■ **WWW**

A swanky restaurant serving scrumptious French haute cuisine – magnificent dishes made with Korean ingredients.

10 **Din Tai Fung** 딘타이펑
MAP M6 ■ 59–1 Myeongdong ■ 3789 2778 ■ **WWW**

The Seoul branch of this award-winning Taiwanese chain is just as good as the rest. This is the place to pig out on wonderful *xiaolongbao* (soup dumplings).

See map on pp76–7

Places to Shop

1 Shinsegae Department Store 신세계 백화점

The oldest department store in Korea is still one of its best. Clothing from most of Korea's famous designers is on display in the luxury wing, and there are great cafés on site (see p79).

Shinsegae Department Store

2 Dongdaemun Market 동대문 시장

This is a huge market area with high-rise towers, malls, covered arcades, and outdoor shacks, though most shoppers come here for cheap clothing and purses (see p22).

3 Euljiro Underground Shopping Arcade 을지로 지하 쇼핑 아케이드

MAP M5 ▪ 161 Euljiro 2-ga

One of the world's longest shopping arcades, Euljiro is pleasingly retro – particularly the clothing favored by older Koreans.

4 Gwangjang Market 광장 시장

Most come here for the food, though it's also famous for silk and other fabrics. There's a great used-clothing market on the second floor on the western flank (see p23).

5 Lotte Department Store 롯데 백화점

MAP H5 ▪ 1 Sogongdong ▪ 771 2500 ▪ Open 10:30am–8pm daily

A huge department store with an array of Korean clothing labels. The basement has Western food-stuffs.

6 Åland 에이랜드

MAP M6 ▪ 53–6 Myeongdong ▪ 318 7640 ▪ Open 9am–10pm daily

Clothing and footwear on the ground floor, and used and vintage clothing on the top level. In between, there's a range of funky stationery.

7 Kumkang Landrover 랜드로바-명동지점

MAP M6 ▪ Myeondong 33-7 ▪ 777 9485

Landrover has every type of shoe you could desire – from formal shoes to sandals to golf shoes and more. A good assortment of both local and imported brands are available.

8 Donghwa Duty Free 동화면세점

MAP L3 ▪ 211 Sejongno ▪ 399 3000 ▪ Open 9:30am–8:30pm daily

Your flight ticket entitles you to tax benefits when buying alcoholic drinks and cosmetics at this store.

9 Monocollection 모노콜렉션

MAP L5 ▪ City Hall ▪ 310 7539 ▪ Open 9am–9pm daily

This popular fabric brand has stores at the airport and at The Plaza hotel (see p114). It also has some wares in the Yido Pottery shop (see p74).

10 Namdaemun Market 남대문 시장

MAP C3 ▪ 49 Namchangdong ▪ Open noon–5pm daily

A fascinating place with hundreds of stores and stalls selling inexpensive clothing and footwear.

Namdaemun Market

Bars and Cafés

Comfortable armchairs at the trendy and upscale Pierre's Bar

 Pierre's Bar 피에르 바
MAP M5 ■ 35 F Lotte Hotel,
1 Sogongdong ■ 317 7181

A glitzy bar adjoining Pierre Gagnaire
à Séoul (see p81). Try the after-work
special set – a signature cocktail
with a few delectable cakes.

2 Baekseju Maeul
백세주마을
MAP M4 ■ 256 Gwancheoldong
■ 720 0055

This bar specializes in a "draft" version
of Baekseju. It also sells *ihwaju* – a
stronger, thicker version of *makgeolli*.

3 Neurin Maeul 느린 마을
MAP E5 ■ 67 Suhadong
■ 6030 0999

Delectable food, as well as various
varieties of *makgeolli* rice beer from
the eponymous brewery,

4 Mongmyeok Sanbang
몽멱 산방
MAP D3 ■ Namsan ■ 318 4790

This is the top tearoom in town in at
least one sense – it is located among
the pines of Namsan, the small
mountain jutting out of central Seoul.

5 Coffee Bean & Tea Leaf
커피빈 앤 티리프
MAP L4 ■ 84 Taepyeongno
■ 753 2374

One branch of this chain, on the
Seoul Finance Center's second
basement level, boasts a Victoria

Arduino Venus Century espresso
machine, of which only 100 were
ever made.

6 Doldamgil 돌담길
MAP K5 ■ 5–1 Jeongdong

Small café set into the grounds of
Deoksugung palace (see p77).

7 Goyangi Darakbang
고양이 다락방
MAP M5 ■ 51–14 Myeongdong 2-ga
■ 318 3123

You can pet a cat here while drinking
your *macchiato*.

8 Taste of Others
타인의 취향
MAP K4 ■ 1-248 Sinmunno ■ 720 0172

With an outdoor terrace, this classy
bar features an extensive list of wines
and champagnes. You can also try
French delicacies such as *escargots*.

9 Leonidas 레오니다스
MAP M5 ■ 2–1 Myeongdong
■ 318 1312

In addition to authentic Belgian
chocolates, Leonidas offers a
range of coffees.

10 Gildeulyeojigi 길들여지기
MAP K5 ■ 8–11 Jeongdong
■ 319 7083

A café-cum-restaurant with the
usual coffee options, as well as
a few distinctly Korean choices –
try the red-bean latte.

See map on pp76–7 ←

TOP 10 Yongsan and Around

Yongsan is by far the most cosmopolitan district in Seoul, with a truly global array of restaurants and some of the trendiest bars and clubs in the city. Not so long ago, however, its very name had negative connotations – an American military base was established here during the Korean War, and the bars and brothels were frequented by stressed-out soldiers. Nowadays the military presence is dwindling, the brothels have all but disappeared, and the area has some interesting sights on offer, such as the War Memorial, which lies adjacent to the American military base, the Leeum Art Museum, and Korea's National Museum.

National Museum of Korea

AREA MAP OF YONGSAN AND AROUND

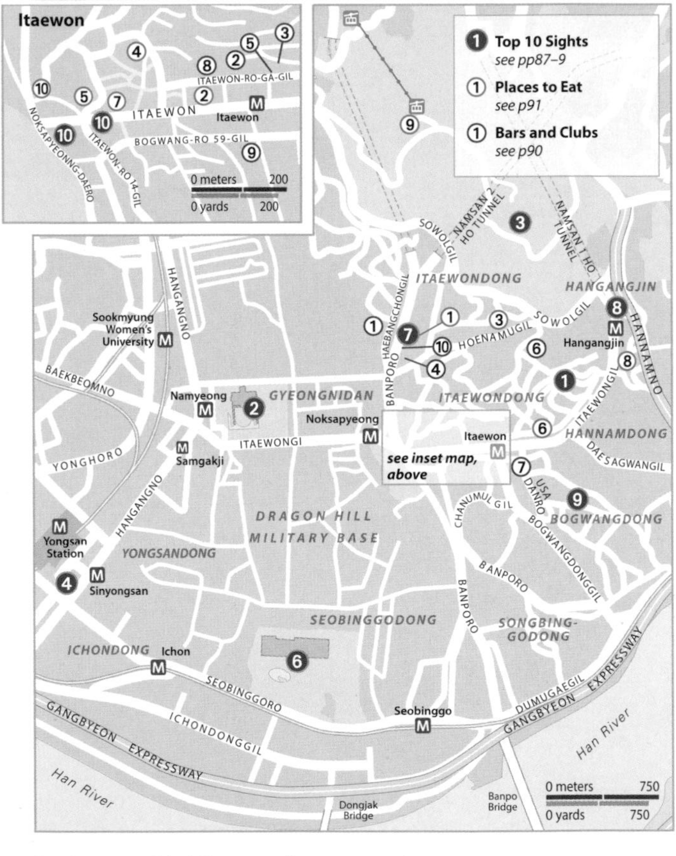

Itaewon

1 Top 10 Sights
see pp87–9

1 Places to Eat
see p91

1 Bars and Clubs
see p90

see inset map, above

1 Leeum, Samsung Museum of Art

삼성미술관 리움
MAP D4 ■ 747–18 Hannamdong
■ 2014 6901 ■ Open 10:30am–6pm
Tue–Sun ■ Adm ■ leeum.
samsungfoundation.org

The Leeum, as it is universally known, is one of the most esteemed museums in the country. Three acclaimed architects – Mario Botta, Rem Koolhaas, and Jean Nouvel – were commissioned to design this project, and the result is a beautiful symphony of architectural styles. The museum is split into several halls, each with its own distinctive and original design. Unfortunately, tickets are often valid only for a specific window of time, and there are extremely strict restrictions on photography – check the museum website for more information.

2 War Memorial of Korea

전쟁기념관
MAP C4 ■ 8 Yongsandong 1-ga
■ 709 3139 ■ Open 9am–6pm Tue–Sun ■ www.warmemo.or.kr

Major wars have punctuated Korean history – the civil war in the early 1950s created North Korea and South Korea, two nations that are still in a state of conflict to this day.

War Memorial of Korea

Though warfare may seem a rather morbid subject for a museum, the exhibitions in this large complex are quite absorbing; information on the Korean War is relayed with care, and the main building is surrounded by a whole regiment's worth of planes, rocket launchers, and similar artifacts.

3 Namsan 남산

Rising up to the north of Yongsan is Namsan, a small mountain with various sights which can easily take half a day to explore. On the Yongsan side, the main attractions are a series of mazelike pathways that meander through the woods past small lakes and viewing platforms (see pp24–5).

Steps leading up the 860-ft- (262-m-) high Namsan mountain

Dragon Hill Spa

4 Dragon Hill Spa 드래곤 힐 스파

MAP C4 ■ 40–713 Hangangno 3-ga ■ 797 0002 ■ Adm

The largest and most famous spa in Seoul, this is a delight to visit. Across its six levels, you'll find dozens of pools ranging from freezing cold to boiling hot – some are infused with green tea, ginseng, and other herbs. There are also various steam rooms, including some lined with amethyst and others with traditional Korean mud walls. Should you so desire, you can even take a nap here – there are dark rooms with small sleeping berths, while on-site restaurants and snack bars ensure that you won't go hungry.

HOMOSEXUALITY IN KOREA

Although homosexuality is still often regarded as a "foreign disease" in Korean society, there are signs that the prejudice is slowly decreasing. The best evidence of this is the increasing number of locals – gay and straight alike – visiting the bars of Itaewon's "Homo Hill." Korea's first openly gay celebrity, Hong Seok-cheon, opened a small restaurant here after he came out in 2000 – paving the way for the rest of the gay population in Seoul.

5 Craft Beer

For decades, it was illegal for small-scale breweries to exist in Korea. With the regulatory shackles now off, Seoul is undergoing a sort of real-ale awakening, led by microbreweries such as Craftworks *(see p56)* and Magpie *(see p57)*.

6 National Museum of Korea 국립중앙박물관

Korea was under the control of several kings from 57 BC to 1910, and relics from 2,000 years of dynastic rule are on display in this gigantic museum. Along with the treasures within, the parklike grounds boast various trails centered on a beautiful lake. Located on the other side of the museum is Yongsan Garrison, an American military base *(see pp20–21)*.

National Museum of Korea

7 **Haebangchon** 해방촌
and Gyeongnidan 경리단
MAP Q5

To the west of central Itaewon, Haebangchon and Gyeongnidan are two adjoining areas that are home to many of Seoul's expatriates. Unlike high-rise, high-energy Itaewon, they are essentially typical Seoul neighborhoods with a relaxed, cosmopolitan twist – new bars and restaurants seem to open on a weekly basis.

8 **Blue Square** 블루 스퀘어
MAP S4 ■ 727–56
Hannamdong ■ 1544 1591 ■ Adm

With eight large floors, Blue Square is one of Korea's largest performance venues. Although the focus is on Korean-language musicals, it also hosts occasional concerts.

Live K-pop at Blue Square

9 **Homo Hill** 호모 힐
MAP S6

A steep side-street running parallel to the main Itaewon street, "Homo Hill" is one of Korea's openly gay areas, and, as such, a trendsetter for Korean gay society as a whole.

10 **Bespoke Tailoring**
MAP R5 ■ Hamilton Shirts: Hamilton Shirts 58–5 Itaewondong; Hanh's Custom Tailoring: 34–16 Itaewondong

Itaewon, a smaller district within Yongsan, is home to an array of tailors, most of whom specialize in making suits and shirts. Compared to international standards, prices here are very low, and though quality varies it can be very high indeed. Hamilton Shirts and Hahn's Custom Tailoring have an excellent reputation.

A DAY IN YONGSAN

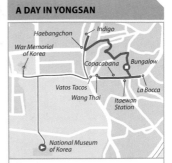

MORNING

Begin the day by visiting the grand **National Museum of Korea**, which is home to thousands of artifacts from Korea's long dynastic history. Two thousand years of regal rule ended with the Japanese occupation, which was almost immediately followed by the catastrophic Korean War in the 1950s. Relics from this conflict are on display in the **War Memorial of Korea** *(see p87)*, just a short taxi ride from the National Museum. Also a short taxi ride away is **Haebangchon**, a trendy district with excellent cafés, which are a boon to those who have spent all morning soaking up history. Try the coffee and cake at **Sugar Daddy** *(see p91)*, before strolling up to Itaewon proper for an early lunch at **Vatos Tacos** *(see p91)*.

AFTERNOON

After lunch, it's time for some shopping. Itaewon has a splendid range of low-cost tailors, with suits and shirts being their specialty. In the evening, head to one of the area's popular restaurants for dinner – choose from a Brazilian barbecue at **Copacabana**, Italian fare at **La Bocca**, or authentic curries at **Wang Thai** *(see p91)*. If you have any energy left, hit the bars and clubs – **District** *(see p90)* is the it-spot, while **The Bungalow** *(see p90)*, with its weird and wonderful seating areas, is one of the quirkiest bars in Seoul.

See map on p86

Bars and Clubs

 Damotori 다모토리
MAP Q4 ■ 44–18 Yongsandong
■ 8950 8362

Sample over 30 varieties of *makgeolli* (*see p57*) in this popular bar. It is mandatory to buy a small meal to go with the drink.

② **District** 디스트릭트
MAP R5 ■ 116–1 Itaewondong
■ 792 6164

With three stylish venues – Prost, Glam, and Club Mute – in one large classy complex, District is one of Itaewon's hottest clubs.

③ **The Bungalow** 더 방갈로
MAP R5 ■ 112–3 Itaewondong
■ 793 2344

A long-running favorite, this bar features quirky seating areas: drink cocktails on a swing, down beers beside an outdoor pool, or sip wine sitting on a rug.

④ **Craftworks Taphouse**
크래프트웍스 탭하우스
MAP Q5 ■ 651 Itaewondong
■ 794 2537

Very popular with local expats, this pub serves a variety of microbrewed beers and excellent grilled food.

All That Jazz

 All That Jazz 올댓재즈
MAP R5 ■ 112–4 Itaewondong
■ 795 5701

This jazz bar opened in 1976 and has hosted most, if not all, Korean jazz artistes of note.

JJ Mahoney's in the Grand Hyatt

⑥ **JJ Mahoney's** JJ 마호니스
MAP S5 ■ 322 Sowollo
■ 799 8601

A lively bar located in the Grand Hyatt, JJ Mahoney's has a dance floor and a poolside terrace with a terrific view of southern Seoul.

⑦ **Hustle** 허슬
MAP R6 ■ 132–3 Itaewondong

Having joined the Itaewon club scene in 2016, Hustle quickly became a go-to venue. DJs will get you into the party mood with a wide variety of music, and be sure to check out their happy hours and special club nights.

⑧ **Fountain** 파운틴
MAP R5 ■ 116–6 Itaewondong

Fountain has three floors: a lounge bar, arcade with pool tables and a VIP area at the top of the building.

⑨ **Gecko's Terrace**
객코스 가든
MAP R5 ■ 128–5 Itaewondong
■ 749 9425

One of Itaewon's older bars, Gecko's Terrace exudes the earthy feel of Itaewon's past – pool, darts, raucous conversations, and cheap draft beer.

⑩ **Magpie** 맥파이
MAP R5 ■ 691 Itaewondong
■ 749 2537

From humble beginnings, the ales produced by this American-run microbrewery are now in demand at expat bars across Korea.

Places to Eat

PRICE CATEGORIES

For the equivalent of a meal for two made up of a range of dishes, or one large dish, with half a bottle of wine.

W under 20,000   **WW** W20,000–100,000
WWW over W100,000

1 Zweiter Stock 츠바이터슈턱
MAP Q5 ▪ 9 Haenamuro 13-gil
▪ 794 9002 ▪ WWW

This German-themed restaurant specializing in lamb dishes is among the best of the many upscale eateries in the area.

2 Copacabana 코파카바나
MAP R6 ▪ 119–9 Itaewondong
▪ 796 1660 ▪ WW

Itaewon now has several *churrascarias* (Brazilian-style steakhouses), but Copacabana was the first, and it remains the best.

3 Sihwadam 시화담
MAP R4 ▪ 5–5 Itaewondong
▪ 798 3311 ▪ WWW

A favorite with dignitaries and businesspeople, this pricey restaurant serves superb food. The courses are gigantic.

4 Sugar Daddy 슈가대디
MAP R5 ▪ 118–5 Itaewondong
▪ 749 0723 ▪ W

Run by Australian-turned-Korean celebrity Sam Hammington, Sugar Daddy satisfies those with a sweet tooth with its colorful cupcakes and desserts.

5 Vatos Tacos 바토스 타코스
MAP R6 ▪ 2nd Floor, 181–8
Itaewondong ▪ 797 8226 ▪ W

Enjoy the Korean-style tacos and chili fries in this eatery.

6 La Bocca 라 보카
MAP S5 ▪ 737–37
Hannamdong ▪ 790 5907 ▪ WW

The pastas and desserts in this Italian are simply fantastic.

7 Wang Thai 왕 타이
MAP Q6 ▪ 176–2 Itaewondong
▪ 749 2746 ▪ W

Don't be fooled by the low-key entrance – both locals and expatriates swear by this modest Thai restaurant.

8 Passion 5 패션 5
MAP S5 ▪ 729–64
Hannamdong ▪ 2071 9505 ▪ W

Indulge in the excellent ice cream and chocolate served in this bakery, the headquarters of the Paris Baguette chain.

Baked goods at Passion 5

9 N Grill 엔 그릴
MAP D3 ▪ N Seoul Tower
▪ 3455 9297 ▪ WWW

Head to this revolving restaurant in N Seoul Tower for splendid 360-degree views of Seoul.

10 Petra 페트라
MAP R5 ▪ 552 Itaewondong
▪ 790 4433 ▪ W

A Jordanian restaurant, Petra has a great range of dips and grilled meats.

See map on p86

TOP10 Western Seoul

Though light on tourist sights, Western Seoul offers an interesting glimpse into contemporary Korean culture. Of particular note is the university belt north of the Han – over 100,000 Seoulites study in these prestigious universities. Upon graduating, many find work in Yeouido, the major financial district in Korea and home to its National Assembly, the largest church in the world, and a fascinating fish market.

Jeoldusan Martyrs' Shrine

1 Sangsangmadang
상상마당

MAP Q2 ▪ 367–5 Seogyodong ▪ 330 6200 ▪ Art market & gallery: open 1–10pm daily; Cinema: open 12:30–8pm daily

This stylish building complex houses a gallery and an art cinema, with installations at the former often governed by what's showing at the latter. There's also a café on the top floor, and a ground-floor shop sells trinkets made by students from the local university.

2 Nightlife

The Hongdae area in Western Seoul has long been Seoul's style lab, particularly in terms of nightlife. This was where Korea's first Western-style

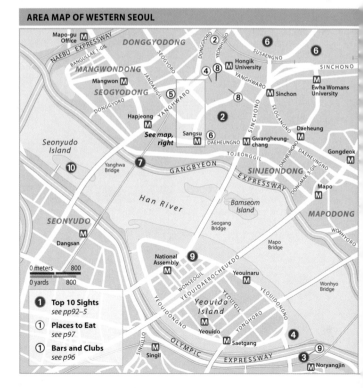

AREA MAP OF WESTERN SEOUL

Stalls of fresh produce at Noryangjin Fisheries Wholesale Market

clubs opened up, while subsequent trends have seen live-music venues, hookah lounges, and microbars open in the area. Hongdae has also been at the forefront of the recent *makgeolli* revolution – head to trendy Wolhyang or Dduk Tak *(see p96)* to try some.

③ Noryangjin Fisheries Wholesale Market
노량진 수산시장

Seoul's largest fish market has not yet found the kind of international fame Tsukiji in Tokyo did, though there's very little difference between the two. The hectic fish auctions make early morning the most interesting time to visit. In the evening, try some of the excellent seafood available in the restaurants located here *(see p97)*.

④ 63 City 63시티
MAP B4 ■ 60 Yeouidodong ■ 789 5663 ■ Open 10am–10pm daily ■ Adm

Seoul's most famous skyscraper, 63 City was built in 1985 on the island of Yeouido. Standing at a height of 820 ft (250 m), it was, on completion, the tallest building outside North America – hard to believe, given the new heights reached by skyscrapers built more recently in Dubai, Hong Kong, Shanghai, and countless other cities. Apart from the viewing platform, which is also an art gallery of sorts, there's the superb 63 World aquarium in the basement levels of the complex.

63 City skyscraper

Hongdae

YANGHWARO / YANGHWA-RO 6-GIL
HONGIK-RO 5-GIL
HONGIK-RO
HONGIK-RO SAN GIL
HONGIKRO 3-GIL
WAUSAN-RO 21-GIL
JANDARI-RO 6-GIL
HONGDAE
JANDARI-RO 2-GIL
WAUSAN-RO 19-GIL
WAUSAN-RO
EOULMADANG-RO
JANDARIG-RO
JANDARI-RO 2-GIL
JANDARIG-RO
EOULMADANG-RO
WAUSAN-RO 17-GIL
DONGMAK-RO 9-GIL
WAUSAN-RO 15-GIL
EOULMADANG-RO
WAUSAN-RO 13-GIL
WAUSANGIL
0 meters   100
0 yards   100
DONGMAK-RO
Sangsu

5 **Luxury Su** 럭셔리 수 노래방
MAP Q2 ■ 367–39 Seogyodong

Karaoke bars are even more popular in Korea than in their homeland of Japan – rare is the road that doesn't have at least one *noraebang* (singing room). Given their ubiquitous nature, few *noraebang* have achieved particular fame, but Luxury Su is a major exception to the rule. Rooms here have been artistically decorated, and those at the front of the building have huge windows, making a rather public display of their patrons' singing.

6 **Two Universities**
MAP B2 ■ Yonsei University: 50 Yonseiro; 3277 2114 ■ MAP B2 ■ Ewha Womans University: 11–1 Daehyeondong; 1599 1885

These two universities of Western Seoul are interesting sights in their own right, with their park-like campuses and strong sense of history. Yonsei University was established in 1885 and Ewha Womans University the following year, and some of the main buildings that are dotted across these two pleasant campuses have survived both the tumultuous years of dynastic rule by Korea's monarchs and of modern, Western-style experimentation.

UNIVERSITY LIFE

Most Koreans attend institutes of higher education, and competition for university seats in Seoul is quite intense. As a result, many children attend academies from the age of 5, their evenings and weekends monopolized by study. However, once they're at a university, they let their hair down – almost every university is surrounded by bars, restaurants, karaoke rooms, and love motels.

7 **Jeoldusan Martyrs' Shrine** 절두산 순교성지
MAP A3 ■ 96–1 Hapjeongdong ■ 312 4434

Though Christianity is now Korea's main religion, Christians were once actively persecuted in the country. Nine French missionaries were executed in 1866, which prompted a purge of local Catholic converts. Many were beheaded on the small cliff of Jeoldusan, on which a shrine has now been built in memorial. Mother Teresa and Pope John Paul II visited the shrine in the 1980s to pay their respects.

Jeoldusan Martyrs' Shrine

8 **Coffee Culture**
Korean coffee culture took off in Western Seoul's university district – Starbucks opened its first Korean branch near Ewha Womans

Ivy-clad Yonsei University

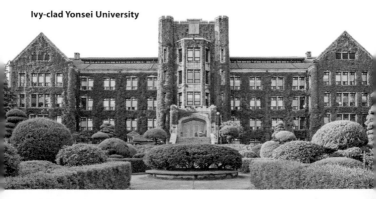

University in 1999. Though café chains still proliferate, there are plenty of independent cafés in the university area, most pertinently Café aA and Coffee Lab *(see p97)*, both located just outside Hongdae.

Yoido Full Gospel Church

9 Yoido Full Gospel Church
여의도 순복음 교회
MAP A4 ■ **11 Yeouidodong**
■ **782 4851** ■ **www.english.fgtv.com**

Yeouido holds one record – the world's largest church. Though the structure itself is smaller than other churches around the world, Yeouido's Full Gospel Church has a membership of over 100,000. There are seven Sunday services held here, and each is translated into over a dozen languages. Regardless of your religious sentiments, visiting is an unusual and interesting experience.

10 Seonyudo 선유도
MAP A3

This small, park-like islet, located in the Han River, makes it possible for visitors to have a Seoul getaway without having to leave the city at all. For decades, Seonyudo was home to the city's main water-treatment plant. Now, however, substantial gentrification has taken place, and visitors are far more likely to notice plants of a greener kind, some of which have grown over the old machinery.

A DAY IN WESTERN SEOUL

▶ MORNING

Those who are able to haul themselves out of bed before the break of dawn should head over to **Noryangjin Fisheries Wholesale Market** *(see p93)* to see its fascinating daily fish auction. If you aren't an early riser, start your day at Yeouido with coffee and a pastry before catching the splendid city views from the top of the **63 City** building *(see p93)*. Afterward, drop by the excellent aquarium in the basement. If it's a Sunday, get yourself over to the **Yoido Full Gospel Church** – with more than 100,000 members, it is the largest church in the world.

AFTERNOON

The winding pathways of **Seonyudo** island are ideal for a long afternoon walk. You can also visit the riverside **Jeoldusan Martyrs' Shrine**. After experiencing the peace and quiet of these two places, liven up your evening by visiting Hongdae, Korea's most entertaining nightlife zone. Try some street snacks *(see p97)* and head to one of the many bars in the area. **Club Evans** and **Drug** *(see p96)* are excellent for live music, while popular **Thursday Party** *(see p96)* is a great place for a group night out. For interesting and fun versions of *makgeolli*, the local rice wine popular with visitors to the city, stop by hip **Wolhyang** or **Dduk Ttak** *(see p96)*. You can also grab a cocktail-to-go from **Vinyl** *(see p96)*.

See map on pp92–3 ←

Bars and Clubs

A jazz quintet performing live at the atmospheric Club Evans

1 Club Evans 클럽 에반스
MAP R3 ▪ 407–3 Seogyodong ▪ 337 8361

One of Korea's best jazz bars, Club Evans hosts two sets each night. The more accomplished ensembles are usually saved for weekends.

2 Thursday Party 써쓰데이 파티
MAP R2 ▪ 364–3 Seogyodong ▪ 324 6621

Packed on weekend nights, this spacious yet bustling bar is a good option for a group night out.

3 Drug 드럭
MAP Q2 ▪ 395–17 Seogyodong ▪ 322 3792

One of the catalysts behind the Seoul indie music scene during the 1990s, Drug is a great bar to hang out in. Gigs take place roughly once a week.

4 Vinyl 비닐
MAP R3 ▪ 411–1 Seogyodong ▪ 322 4161

This small bar serves cocktails in vinyl pouches. There are only a couple of tables here, so most customers take their drinks away with them.

5 Wolhyang 월향
MAP S1 ▪ 352–23 Seogyodong ▪ 324 1180

A trendy *makgeolli* bar, Wolhyang prides itself on a version made with "unwashed" brown rice.

6 Bar Da 바다
MAP R3 ▪ 365-12 Seogyodong ▪ 337 1818

This unpretentious bar in the hectic Hongdae neighborhood is a great spot for a drink and a chat.

7 Ho Bar 호 바
MAP A3 ▪ Ho Bar 3: B1 358–1 Seogyodong ▪ 336 6011

This chain of bars is a phenomenon – at the last count, there were more than 10 in the Hongdae area. Ho Bar 3, downhill from the Hongik university entrance, is usually the busiest.

8 Dduk Tak 뚝닥
MAP A3 ▪ 330–17 Seogyodong ▪ 336 6883

A great example of a "fun" *makgeolli* bar. With flavors like banana, kiwi, honey, and even tomato on offer, the *makgeolli* here is not exactly Korean, but tasty nonetheless.

9 NB 엔비
MAP R2 ▪ 362–4 Seogyodong ▪ 326 1716

A gigantic hip-hop club, NB has DJs playing the latest hits. It is best to get here early to avoid the queue.

10 Mansion 맨션
MAP Q2 ▪ 368–22 Seogyodong ▪ 3143 4037

A trendy lounge bar on weekdays, Mansion is very popular with students on weekend nights.

Places to Eat

PRICE CATEGORIES

For the equivalent of a meal for two made up of a range of dishes, or one large dish, with half a bottle of wine.

W under W20,000 **WW** W20,000–100,000 **WWW** over W100,000

1 **Café aA** 카페 aA
MAP Q3 ■ 408–11 Seogyodong
■ 3143 7312 ■ W

This café has one of Korea's finest furniture collections *(see p54)*.

Coffee-drinkers ar Café aA

2 **Yeonamm Terrace**
연남테라스
MAP R1 ■ 228–7 Yeonnamdong
■ 3144 6804 ■ W

A talented young Korean chef presents innovative Western dishes.

3 **Bukchon Sonmandu**
북촌손만두
MAP Q2 ■ 405–14 Seogyodong
■ 555 1000 ■ W

A shack which serves a range of cheap dumplings. Its picture menus make ordering a simple affair.

4 **Saemaeul Sikdang**
새마을식당
MAP A3 ■ 331–18 Seogyodong
■ 332 0120 ■ W

This BBQ-meat restaurant chain offers high-quality meat at low prices.

5 **Julio** 후리오
MAP A3 ■ 411–18 Seogyodong
■ 3141 5324 ■ WW

Mexican food is rarely authentic in Seoul. Julio is a cut above the norm.

6 **Tong Tong Pig** 통통돼지
MAP R3 ■ 309–3 Sangsudong
■ 325 6007 ■ W

Fuel up on barbecued pork at Tong Tong Pig before hopping over to the Hongdae for the vibrant nightlife.

7 **Street Food**
MAP R2 ■ W

The Hongdae area is packed with vendors serving cheap snacks to hungry students. The T-junction near Sangsu station has street vendors selling fried, battered, tempura-like snacks known as *twigim*.

8 **Coffee Lab** 커피 랩
MAP S1 ■ 327–19 Seogyodong
■ 3143 0908 ■ W

This serves excellent coffee using a variety of beans, roasting imple-ments, and extraction methods.

9 **Noryangjin Fisheries Wholesale Market**
노량진 수산시장
MAP B5 ■ 13–8 Noryangjindong
■ 814 2211 ■ WW

Seoul's fish market has a few restaurants where you can order from the menu, or bring your purchases from the market to be cooked.

Noryangjin Wholesale Market

10 **Fell & Cole** 팰앤콜
MAP Q3 ■ 7 Seopyeongdaero 8-gil ■ 4411 1434 ■ W

By far the best ice cream in Seoul. It's a little hard to find, but gelato flavors such as fig mascarpone, carrot cake, and salted caramel are reward for such effort.

See map on pp92–3 ←

TOP 10 Southern Seoul

For much of Seoul's time as capital of the Joseon kingdom (1392–1910), the whole city was located north of the river, in a tight area between the Bugaksan and Namsan mountains. The baby boom that followed the Korean War, and the economic boom after that, resulted in a rapid expansion of the city, now leaving the southern half even more populous than the north. It is well worth crossing the river to see an area that feels like a window into the Korea of the future.

Burial mounds and tombs in Seonjeongneung cemetery

AREA MAP OF SOUTHERN SEOUL

Seonjeongneung 선정릉
MAP F5 ▪ 135–4
Samseongdong ▪ Open Mar–Oct:
9am–6:30pm Tue–Sun; Nov–Feb:
9am–5:30pm Tue–Sun ▪ Adm

The royals of dynastic Korea were buried with their possessions in large mounds of earth – a far simpler and more natural version of the pyramids of Egypt. The tombs in this calm, tree-filled place are the ones most accessible for visitors to Seoul – this was the burial site for two kings and one queen from the Joseon dynasty. The queen in question, Jeonghyeon (1462–1530), is said to have founded the nearby temple of Bongeunsa.

2 **Garosugil** 가로수길
MAP E4

Its name translates as "tree-lined road," and Garosugil is, indeed, lined with gingko trees. A once nondescript road, it has been transformed into one of the trendiest parts of Seoul and has an ever-changing roster of cafés, boutiques, and restaurants.

3 **Gwacheon** 과천

A half-hour subway ride from Central Seoul, the neighboring city of Gwacheon is markedly different in feel from the capital. It boasts a number of interesting sights, including Seoul Grand Park, the National Museum of Contemporary Art, Gwacheon National Science Museum, and Seoul Race Park. Gwacheon is also home to Seoul Land amusement park, the widest swath of parkland in Seoul, and there are a few hiking trails in the nearby mountains (see pp34–5).

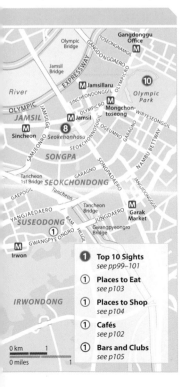

Bongeunsa temple

4 **Bongeunsa** 봉은사
MAP F5 ▪ 73 Samseongdong
▪ 511 6070 ▪ Open 3–10pm daily

One of urban Seoul's few major Buddhist temples, Bongeunsa is even more attractive than Jogyesa, its north-of-the-river counterpart (see p16). When looking north from the entrance, visitors can see a steep hill dotted with colorful wooden structures; if they look the other way from the top, they will see nothing but high-rise buildings – the rather interesting contrast of traditional and modern Seoul.

0 km   1
0 miles   1

Seoul National Cemetery

5 Seoul National Cemetery 국립현충원

MAP C5 ■ San 44–7 Dongjakdong ■ 813 9625 ■ Open Mar–Oct: 6am–8pm daily, Nov–Feb: 7am–5pm Sun–Fri

This cemetery is of major historical importance. It is the resting place of three former presidents: Seungman Lee (Syngman Rhee), the country's first leader; Park Chung-hee, a dictatorial ruler, yet the catalyst for Korea's economic turnaround; and Kim Dae-jung, winner of the 2000 Nobel Peace prize.

6 Samsung d'light 삼성 딜라이트

MAP E6 ■ Samsung Electronics Building, 1320–10 Seochodong ■ 2255 2262 ■ Open 10am–7pm Mon–Fri

Although Gangnam station is surrounded by neon-lit streets and has many restaurants, bars, and

Theme park at Lotte World

cafés, there is little of note to tourists in the area, except the headquarters of Samsung Electronics – the most important wing of Korea's world-famous corporation. A few of the lower floors have been converted into a fascinating showroom of past, present, and future Samsung gadgets, and feature plenty of interactive, hi-tech displays.

7 Coex Mall 코엑스 몰

MAP F5 ■ 159 Samseongdong ■ Aquarium: 6002 6200; open 10am–pm daily; adm ■ Pulmuone Kimchi Museum: 6002 6546; open 10am–6pm Tue–Sun; adm ■ www.coex.co.kr

Seoul's main shopping mall, Coex is an entirely underground affair, and a highly popular rainy-day magnet for Seoulites. For those who'd like to do something other than shop, there is a huge aquarium as well as the Pulmuone Kimchi Museum, the best place for visitors to learn how to make Korea's most famous dish.

8 Lotte World 롯데 월드

MAP H5 ■ 40–1 Jamsildong ■ 411 2000 ■ Open 9:30am–10pm daily ■ Adm

The gigantic Lotte World complex is a real favorite with the young and young-at-heart alike. Most come for the theme park, which is split into indoor and outdoor sections – the indoor component weaves in and out of a large shopping mall, while the outdoor section is arranged around an artificial lake. There's also a folk museum and an ice-skating rink.

KOREAN BURIAL MOUNDS

Since time immemorial, Koreans have buried their dead in grass-covered mounds of earth. The rapid urbanization of the country has made this an extremely expensive practice – prohibitively so in Seoul. The Seonjeongneung and the Seoul National Cemetery are striking examples of this tradition.

Banpo Bridge at night

9 Banpo Bridge 반포 대교
MAP D5

By day, Banpo Bridge is just one of two dozen bridges straddling the Hangang, the river that bisects Central Seoul. In the evening, however, each side of the bridge is lined with high-pressure water jets, which essentially make a centipede-shaped fountain of the entire structure. The display is illuminated with thousands of LEDs, making for one of Seoul's more memorable nighttime experiences.

10 Seoul Olympic Park
서울 올림픽 공원
MAP H4 ■ 88 Bangidong ■ 410 1114
■ Olympic Park: Open 6am–10pm daily; Olympic Museum: Open 10am–6pm Tue–Sun

Seoul hosted the Summer Olympics in 1988 (see p39), and venues from the games are still in use today. This park is one of the best places in Seoul for an afternoon stroll, and on weekends it often hosts community events. The Olympic Museum located in the park is also interesting.

A DAY IN SOUTHERN SEOUL

▶ MORNING

Begin your day with a cup of good coffee at **The Lounge** (see p102) – a snazzy café set atop the Park Hyatt. You can also try one of their signature smoothies. Afterward, the remainder of the morning can be spent soaking up a bit of Korean culture. The Buddhist temple of **Bongeunsa** (see p99) offers great opportunities for photographs, while the **Seonjeongneung** (see p99) – the royal burial mounds located next to the Seonjeongneung subway station – are both educational about local history and perfect for a morning walk.

AFTERNOON

Head over to trendy **Garosugil** (see p99) for lunch – try some delicious gimbap (a traditional Korean rice snack) with different toppings at **Lee's Gimbap** (see p103). Then it's time to hit the area's shops. There are plenty in Garosugil itself, but label-hunters should head over to **Apgujeong** (not far from the Apgujeong Rodeo subway station) for the flagship stores of major international labels (see p112). The side-streets around **Dosan Park** (see p104) are known for their small but quirky boutiques. If you are tired after all the shopping, make your way to the nearby **Philkyungjae** (see p103), where you can dine like a Korean king. After that, it'll be time to get yourself over to **Banpo Bridge** – straddling the Han River, this structure turns into a giant, spectacular fountain as night approaches.

See map on pp98–9 ←

Cafés

1 **Café Madang** 카페 마당
MAP E4 ■ 630–26 Sinsadong
■ 3015 3208
This attractive, chic café is located in the basement of the Hermès building in Apgujeong.

2 **Han River Bridge Cafés**
Six bridges over the Han River have small, quirky cafés at their southern ends. All offer great views of the river.

3 **Monk to Bach** 몽크투바흐
MAP E4■ 564–9 Sinsadong
■ 8637 5636
Named for the legendary pianist Thelonious Monk and Baroque master Johannes Bach, the café has state-of-the-art speakers and more than 16,000 albums - basically heaven for jazz and classical music aficionados!

4 **Coffee Smith** 커피 스미스
MAP E5 ■ 536–20 Sinsadong
■ 3445 3372
One of the larger cafés in Seoul, Coffee Smith is spread over two levels; three in summer, when tables and chairs spill onto the street.

5 **74**
MAP E4 ■ 83–20
Cheongdamdong ■ 542 7412
With its bright interior, 74 is popular from late morning to late evening. It serves a wide range of light meals, plus teas and ice creams.

Modern interior of the Lounge

6 **The Lounge** 더라운지
MAP F5 ■ 2016 1205
In the Park Hyatt hotel *(see p114)*, The Lounge offers superb views of Seoul and has great desserts. Try *patbingsu* – a Korean sweet made with cream, ice shavings, and fruity toppings.

7 **Café Slow** 카페 슬로우
MAP E5■ 1308–12
Seochodong ■ 3482 0111
A licensed café-cum-bar, this is one of the few places in Gangnam offering shisha.

8 **Miel** 미엘
MAP E4 ■ 94–3
Cheongdamdong ■ 512 2395
With a range of comfy seats arranged around honeycomb-like slats and hexagons, Miel has the appearance of a giant beehive. It serves excellent drinks.

9 **Baek Eok Café** 백억 카페
MAP F5 ■ 618–11
Yeoksamdong ■ 568 7788
This large, trendy café's name hints at the affluence of the Gangnam area – *baek* is the Korean word for "100" and *eok* the term for "100 million."

10 **10 Corso Como**
10 꼬르소 꼬모
MAP E4 ■ 79 Cheongdamdong
■ 547 3010
Seoul's branch of the Milanese designer label comes with its own chic café and is extremely popular.

Counter area at 74

Places to Eat

PRICE CATEGORIES
For the equivalent of a meal for two made up of a range of dishes, or one large dish, with half a bottle of wine.

W under W20,000 WW W20,000–100,000
WWW over W100,000

1 Philkyungjae 필경재
MAP G6 ▪ 739–1 Suseodong
▪ 445 2115 ▪ WW

Based in a 500-year-old building, this restaurant serves Korean royal cuisine. Many of their set menus are for three people or more.

2 Crystal Jade Palace
크리스탈 제이드 팰리스
MAP F5 ▪ 159–7 Samseongdong
(10th Floor) ▪ 3288 8101 ▪ WWW

One of the city's top restaurants, this place serves a mix of Cantonese and Shanghainese specialties.

3 Yu Ga Ne 유가네
MAP F5 ▪ 817–10 Yeoksamdong
▪ 563 3392 ▪ WW

An inexpensive option, Yu Ga Ne serves delicious *dak-galbi*, a spicy chicken and lettuce dish, made in front of you at your table.

4 Isabelle the Butcher
이사벨더부처
MAP D5 ▪ 118–3 Banpodong
▪ 535 9820 ▪ WW

One of the first restaurants in Korea to serve dry-aged beef, this is a must-visit for meat connoisseurs.

5 Tutto Bene 투토 베네
MAP E4 ▪ 118–9
Cheongdamdong ▪ 546 1489 ▪ WW

Superb pasta dishes served in a romantic setting – this Italian restaurant is a must-visit.

6 Oga No Kitchen 오가노주방
MAP E5 ▪ 645–8 Sinsadong
▪ 514 0058 ▪ WW

A Japanese-Korean restaurant offering a variety of sakes and organic fusion dishes.

7 Lee's Gimbap 리김밥
MAP E5 ▪ 610 Sinsadong
▪ 548 5552 ▪ W

At the lowest end of the price spectrum in Gangnam, this tiny place serves artisanal versions of *gimbap* – the regular snack of rice in lavered seaweed, but here it comes stuffed with treats like Gouda cheese or shiitake mushrooms.

8 Bamboo House
뱀부 하우스
MAP F5 ▪ 658–10 Yeoksamdong
▪ 566 0870 ▪ WW

Specializing in barbecued meat, Bamboo House has multilingual staff, easy-to-read menus, and an excellent wine list.

Cozy interiors of the Melting Shop

9 Melting Shop 멜팅샵
MAP E4 ▪ 647–19 Sinsadong
▪ 544 4256 ▪ WW

An excellent retro-styled diner near Dosan Park, the menu consists of a handful of perfected specialties. Reservations recommended.

10 Tang 땅
MAP F5 ▪ 601–1 Yeoksamdong
▪ 554 0707 ▪ WW

An attractive Vietnamese restaurant, Tang is most popular with diners for its *salguksu* – a local version of Vietnam's famous pho noodle soup.

See map on pp98–9

Places to Shop

1 **Garosugil** 가로수길
MAP E4
Dotted with gingko trees, Garosugil
has long been one of Seoul's most
fashionable thoroughfares.

2 Boon the Shop 분 더 샵
MAP E4 ■ 89 Cheongdamdong
■ 2056 1234
A stylish luxury mall, this stocks
top local brands and a smattering
of international labels. The main
foyer functions as an art exhibition
space of sorts.

Airy Times Square mall

3 **Times Square** 타임 스퀘어
MAP A5 ■ 442 Yeongdeungpo-
dong ■ 2638 2000
A large mall, Times Square has most
international high-street labels as
well as a selection of local chains.

**4 Maison de Lee Young
Hee** 이영희한복집
MAP E5 ■ 665–5 Sinsadong
■ 547 0630
This boutique is owned by renowned
Korean designer Lee Young Hee,
who is known for creating contemporary and wearable styles of the
hanbok – Korea's national dress.

5 Designer Stores
디자이너 스토어
MAP E5
A few high-end stores in the
Dosan Park area were designed by
prominent architects – check out the
space-age local flagship store of the
Belgian label Ann Demeulemeester.

6 Dosan Park Boutiques
도산공원 부띠끄
MAP E5 ■ 649–9 Sinsadong
If you are looking for local brands, try
the small side-streets around Dosan
Park to stumble upon its many
charming boutiques.

7 Daily Projects
데일리 프로젝트
MAP E4 ■ 1–24 Cheongdamdong
■ 3218 4072
This small and stylish shop has
a great selection of brands from
mostly up-and-coming local
designers. They hold a flea
market on Sundays.

8 Galleria 겔러리아 백화점
MAP F4 ■ 515 Apgujeongdong
■ 3449 4114
Regarded as the most luxurious
department store in Seoul, Galleria
has a great selection of major labels.

9 Coex Mall 코엑스 몰
MAP F5 ■159 Samseongdong
■ 6000 1162
In addition to an array of shops
and restaurants, this underground
mall also has the interesting
Pulmuone Kimchi Museum to
entertain visitors (see p99).

**10 Homeplus Smart
Virtual Store**
홈 플러스 스마트 가상 스토어
Connected to the Seoulleung subway
station, this is a virtual store.
Customers can register and buy
goods with their cell phones after
selecting them from flat-screen
images arranged like two-
dimensional goods racks.

Bars and Clubs

Upscale Timber House bar at the Park Hyatt hotel

1 **Timber House** 팀버 하우스
MAP F6 ■ 2016 1234
Located in the Park Hyatt *(see p114)* this traditional bar offers a great selection of Japanese sake.

2 **Moon Jar** 달빛술담 문자르
MAP E5 ■ 644–19 Sinsadong ■ 541 6118
The best and most popular *makgeolli* bar south of the Han River, Moon Jar offers a country-wide selection of the milky rice wine, plus an excellent range of fruity cocktails.

3 **Once in a Blue Moon**
원스인어블루문
MAP F4 ■ 824 Seolleungno ■ 549 5490
Nightly shows by top musicians at this renowned Gangnam jazz bar are of a uniformly high quality.

4 **Club Ellui** 클럽 엘루이
MAP E4 ■ 129
Cheongdamdong ■ 9111 6205
This popular party spot can accommodate over 4,000 people.

5 **Le Chamber** 르 챔버
MAP F5 ■ 83–4
Cheongdamdong ■ 6337 2014
If you're tired of gulping down the same drinks all the time, head to Le Chamber for unique cocktails such as Chung Dam Zombie.

6 **Rainbow** 레인보우
MAP D6 ■ 1308–11
Seochodong ■ 3481 1869
Leave your shoes at the door. Once inside this laid-back place, relax on the floor cushions while listening to mellow tunes and perhaps enjoying a hookah.

7 **Club Base** 클럽 베이스
MAP F5 ■ 602 Yeoksamdong ■ 6447 0042 ■ www.clubbase.net
Colorful seats and illuminated drinks counters make this club, tucked under the Ritz-Carlton hotel, a favorite with Seoul's young crowd.

8 **Coffee Bar K** 커피 바 K
MAP E4 ■ 675–3 Yeoksamdong ■ 318 1570
This cozy bar has hundreds of varieties of whiskey to choose from.

9 **Club Answer** 클럽 앤써
MAP E4 ■ 125–16
Cheongdamdong ■ 514 4311
Everyone wants to get onto the VIP level at this super exclusive club.

10 **Syndrome** 신드롬
MAP E5 ■ 587-1 Sinsadong ■ 544 7227
Specializing in electronica, this is the only club in Seoul to include an on-site swimming pool.

See map on pp98–9

Streetsmart

**A traditional Korean street
in Bukchon Hanok Village**

Getting To and Around Seoul

Arriving by Air

Incheon International Airport [see p42] is one of the best in the world, and it has been the recipient of numerous international awards. Direct, nonstop flights link it with pretty much every major city in Europe, North America, Asia, and Australasia – often with a combination of national flag-carriers and one or both of Korea's own airlines, **Korean Air** and **Asiana**. From Europe, it's often cheaper to fly via the Middle East or Russia; from Australia, you can usually save money by taking a combination of budget airlines through Southeast Asia.

There are two main methods of getting from the airport to central Seoul: bus and rail. Most visitors take the bus – there are 15 separate routes into the capital (W10,000), as well as "limousine" buses (W15,000), which head directly to many of the major hotels. The airport's tourist booths (of which there are many) will be able to advise on which service is best for you; most buses depart every 15 minutes or so, and take 50–90 minutes, depending on where you're headed.

Taking the **AREX** train is cheaper (around W4,000), and it can save you time if you're going to the city centre (56 minutes to Seoul station). Note that the "express" services (around W9,000) only shave 10 minutes

or so off the journey, but they are far more comfortable.

Lastly, taxis will cost W80,000–140,000 into Seoul, depending on the destination, time of day, and prevailing traffic.

There's also a second major airport, located halfway between Incheon and central Seoul: **Gimpo International Airport** is mainly used for domestic flights but also some services from Asia. The airport is also on the AREX train route into Seoul (although express services do not stop here), as well as subway line 5; many airport buses from Incheon also stop here on their way into Seoul.

Arriving by Sea

There are ferries to Incheon, a city west of Seoul, from a dozen ports on the east Chinese coast. Most services run two or three times per week, and they take between 16 and 24 hours to arrive, depending on the city of departure. The closest port to Beijing is Tanggu, which is a taxi ride from Tianjin city and served by direct high-speed trains from Beijing. From Japan, there are ferries most days from Fukuoka and Shimonoseki to Busan (7 hours), in Korea's southeastern corner and around 3 hours from Seoul by high-speed train. Faster and more regular (though less pleasant) are the several daily catamaran departures linking Busan and Fukuoka (3 hours).

Arriving by Train

There are no international trains to Seoul – South Korea's only international land border is with North Korea, and this has been off-limits to travelers for decades. Most domestic services, run by **Korail**, terminate at **Seoul** or **Yongsan** stations, both centrally located on subway lines 1 and 4. A few services from the east terminate at Cheongnyangni station, also on line 1. There are several classes of train, with the fastest being the KTX high-speed services, for which prices rise slightly at weekends; this is the fastest way to and from Suwon.

Arriving by Bus

Seoul's two main bus terminals are the **Express Bus Terminal** (also known as Gangnam Bus Terminal), south of the river, on subway lines 3, 7, and 9; and the **Dong-Seoul Bus Terminal**, east of the center, next to Gangbyeon subway station (line 2). There are regular bus services to every city in the land.

Getting Around by Subway

Seoul's subway is one of the most comprehensive on earth, with 18 lines and counting. Despite its unwieldy size, the system is excellent – trains arrive with unerring frequency and almost never break down. In addition, there is English-language signage in trains and stations alike, and visitors will find street maps (also with English-language text) of the surrounding area by most subway exits.

Ticket prices on the Seoul subway start at W1,150 per journey, and rarely rise above W2,000 – travelers will save money as well as time if they buy a ticket from the slightly confusing machines using a T-Money transport card.

Many of the destinations described in the Seoul excursions section *(see pp64–5)* are accessible by subway, including Incheon, Suwon, Everland and Yangsu-ri.

Getting Around by Bus

Unless travelers are able to read and understand Korean, the city's bus system is likely to prove a bit tricky to use, although with decent guidance it will get you wherever you want to go. City bus ticket prices start at W1,050, although note that these are cashless affairs – you can only pay by T-Money transport card.

Getting Around by Taxi

Travelers will rarely be too far from a taxi in Seoul. The starting rate is W3,000 and, unless you're heading far across the city, you will most likely receive change from W10,000. Prices rise by 20 percent after midnight, and the black "luxury" cabs – most commonly found lying in wait around the higher-end hotels – cost around 50 percent more. Most taxis accept credit cards and T-Money transport cards.

Taxi drivers are almost uniformly trustworthy, especially with foreign passengers. Although few can speak English, most have been trained to access an interpreter via their in-car phones, should the need arise – a free service that is encouraged by the city and national authorities.

Tickets and Transport Cards

Single-use tickets for the subway can be purchased from machines inside the stations, for a refundable deposit of W500. It's far better to get a T-Money transport card, for a refundable deposit of W3,000, from the same machines – you'll save time and W100 per sub-way journey.

In addition, a T-Money transport card is the only way to travel on city buses. You can also use them to pay in taxis and convenience stores, as well as make calls from many public telephones.

Getting Around on Foot

Seoul isn't exactly a pedestrian's paradise, with drivers regularly flouting rules of the road, and many sidewalks (on those roads lucky enough to have them) becoming parking spaces or motor-bike routes. However, the city center is relatively straightforward to get around on foot – it is possible to stroll between most of the main sights described in the Palace Quarter *(see pp68–75)* and Central Seoul *(see pp76–83)* chapters of this book.

DIRECTORY

AIRPORTS

Gimpo International Airport
☎ 1661 2626
🌐 airport.co.kr

Incheon International Airport
☎ 1577 2600
🌐 airport.kr

AIRLINES

Asiana
🌐 flyasiana.com

Korean Air
🌐 koreanair.com

TRAINS

AREX (airport rail)
🌐 arex.or.kr

Korail (national rail)
🌐 letskorail.com

Seoul Station
MAP C3
◾ 405 Hoehyeondong, Seoul
☎ 3149 2522

Yongsan Station
MAP C4
◾ Hangangdaero, Seoul
☎ 1544 7788

BUSES

Dong-Seoul Bus Terminal
MAP G4
◾ 546 Gueuidong, Seoul
☎ 1688 5979

Express Bus Terminal
MAP D5
◾ 162 Banpodong, Seoul
☎ 535 4151

Bus Schedule Information
☎ 060 305 070
🌐 www.kobus.co.kr

Practical Information

Passports and Visas

Citizens of more than 100 nations – including the US, Canada, Australia, New Zealand, and most of Europe – are granted visa-free entry on arrival. The period allowed in the country varies from one to six months – 90 days is most common, but check with your local South Korean embassy. Keep your passport with you at all times to serve as identification.

Customs Regulations

Getting through the gates at Incheon International Airport is generally a breeze – lines tend to be short and customs officials efficient. A quirk of the local system is that you're only allowed to bring in one bottle of alcohol, whether a bottle of beer or a huge bottle of spirits. Travelers carrying more than US$10,000 in cash must declare the amount on arrival. Check **Korea Customs Service** for more information.

Penalties for carrying drugs can be severe – you can be prosecuted for having traces of certain chemicals in your system.

Travel Safety Advice

Visitors can get up-to-date travel safety information from the **Foreign and Commonwealth Office** in the UK, the **State Department** in the US, and the **Department of Foreign Affairs and Trade** in Australia.

Travel Insurance

It is unwise to travel without valid insurance, particularly in Seoul, due to the cost of local healthcare. Be sure to check the specifics of your current policy, especially whether or not it covers travel to South Korea – although it is a safe country, some policies do not.

Health

No vaccinations are mandatory to visit South Korea. Malaria-carrying mosquitoes occasionally fly across the DMZ from North Korea, although the chances of catching the disease are very low. It is worth bringing along strong repellent for the mosquito-infested fall and summer months.

Most of Seoul's hospitals have English-speaking doctors; **Seoul National University Hospital** also has English-speaking dentists. Travelers to the city will also find hospitals with 24-hour English-language information lines as well as dedicated international clinics, such as **Severance Hospital**.

Pharmacies or *yakguk* can be found on almost every major road. Some are open all night, and most will have at least one English-speaking member of staff on duty. For behind-the-counter medication, you will need a prescription.

The tap water is safe to drink, but few locals ever do. Mineral water is available in convenience stores for a reasonable price.

Personal Security

Crime rates in Seoul are very low for such a large city – a pleasant surprise to most visitors. Petty theft is nearly non-existent, as is drug use (penalties are severe) and its associated social side-effects. If you do run into trouble, call your embassy for advice. The city also presents no particular challenges for female travelers, although some local women are wary of taking taxis alone at night.

Emergency Services

The **fire brigade and ambulance** have a dedicated hotline, as do the **police**. When calling the emergency services, it is usually possible to have your call forwarded to someone who speaks English, but since this can take time, it is best to have a local make the call on your behalf.

Currency and Banking

The national currency is the won (W), which comes in notes of 50,000, 10,000, 5,000, and 1,000 won, and coins of 500, 100, 50, and 10 won (with the latter two used somewhat less frequently). Most banks have international card-friendly ATMs, though connection can be hit and miss – you may have to try a few different banks before finding success. ATMs are usually open around the clock, barring a couple of off-service hours just after midnight.

Credit cards are increasingly accepted in hotels, shops, cafés, restaurants, and taxis. In general, any place that accepts local credit cards will be able to accept foreign ones, too.

Telephone and Internet

Finding Wi-Fi hotspots is usually simple – several major café chains in the capital now offer their customers free Internet access. Most higher-end hotels charge daily fees of around W20,000 for connection; at the other end of the scale, the rooms of many newer motels have Internet-ready computer terminals.

The concept of buying SIM cards alone does not exist in Korea, and unless you have a quad-band handset, it is unlikely that your cell phone will work in Seoul. Check with your service provider before traveling.

Booths at Incheon International Airport rent out cell phones to travelers. If you are staying for any longer than a couple of weeks, it may be cheaper to buy a simple pre-paid handset in Seoul. Although you can register it yourself at a telephone showroom, those who have Korean friends will find it easier to do so with them.

If you are stuck for a call, there are public payphones all over the city (most commonly near the junctions of main roads); all are incredibly cheap, some take coins, and others will work with your T-money transport card *(see p109)*.

Postal Services

There is one post office *(ucheguk)* in each city neighborhood, and you will usually be able to locate your nearest one by looking on the maps that you'll find next to most subway station exits. Most post offices are open 9am–6pm Monday to Friday and 9am–1pm on Saturday. Staff are unlikely to speak English.

Opening Hours

Banks are usually open 9am–4pm Monday to Friday. Most restaurants open up in the morning and close in the late evening, with some even staying open all night. It's certain that as long as you have cash, you won't ever go hungry. In addition, convenience stores are on almost every street, and all are open 24 hours a day, every day of the year.

Most shops open at 9am or 10am, and stay open until late evening, except department stores, which close at around 6pm. Certain parts of Dongdaemun and Namdaemun markets *(for both, see p82)* are open 24 hours a day.

Museums and galleries keep fairly standard international hours – usually 9am–6pm, with a day off on Monday.

Time Difference

South Korea is 17 hours ahead of US West Coast time, 14 hours ahead of US East Coast time, and 9 hours ahead of GMT. Daylight saving time is not used in the country.

Electrical Appliances

Electrical current is 220 volts AC – the same as Europe, but double that in North America. Wall sockets in Seoul also take plugs with two round pins. North American appliances may need a transformer.

DIRECTORY

EMBASSIES

British Embassy
MAP K5 ■ 24
Sejongdaero 19-gil
🌐 gov.uk

US Embassy
MAP L3 ■ 188
Sejongdaero
🌐 seoul.usebmassy.gov

CUSTOMS REGULATIONS

Korea Customs Service
🌐 english.customs.go.kr

TRAVEL SAFETY ADVICE

Australia
🌐 dfat.gov.au
🌐 smartraveller.gov.au

UK
🌐 gov.uk/foreign-travel-advice

US
🌐 travel.state.gov

HEALTH

Seoul National University Hospital
MAP D2 ■ 28
Yeongeondong
📞 2072 2890 / 0505

Severance Hospital
MAP B2 ■ 134
Shinchondong
📞 2228 5800

EMERGENCY SERVICES

Fire Brigade and Ambulance
📞 119

Police
📞 112

TV, Radio, and Newspapers

All hotels offer guests a few international TV channels. In addition, local cable TV chanels occasionally show sub-titled English-language films and programs.

Time, *Newsweek*, and *The Economist* magazines are available in many of the major bookstores. Among the local English-language monthlies, *10 Magazine* and *Seoul Selection* are recom-mended. The two main English-language daily newspapers are *The Korea Times* and *The Korea Herald*.

Weather

Korean summers are hot, wet, and humid – temperatures in Seoul can often soar well over 86° F (30° C) in June and July, which are also the rainiest months of the year. Winter is long and cold – the temperature rarely rises above 32° F (0° C) during December, January, and February, and it can plummet below 5° F (-15° C), though there are blue skies most days. Spring (Apr–Jun) and fall (Sep–Oct) are by far the best seasons to visit the city.

Disabled Travellers

Seoul is not a very wheelchair-friendly place. Many streets have no proper sidewalks, and the sidewalks that do exist are used by motor-bike drivers or parked cars. However, many of the city's subway stations have been specially adapted to make them more accessible (although this is not yet city-wide). Most hotels and museums have lifts, though you will find the occasional entrance that has been built without wheelchairs in mind.

Tourist Information

Information booths can be found at quite a few places around the city. There are also plenty of booths inside Incheon International Airport. The official websites of the **Korea Tourism Organization** and **Seoul Tourism Organization** are excellent sources of travel information.

Trips and Tours

Daily tour buses run between the main sights hourly from 9am to 6pm; night bus tours start at 8pm. There are also 2- to 3-hour-long walking tours of the Palace Quarter. The Seoul Tourism Organization has information on all these tours. The Integrated Palace Ticket for W10,000 includes admission to Jongmyo, Deoksugung, Changgyeonggung, Changdeokgung, and Gyeongbokung, and lasts up to a month.

Shopping

There are surprisingly few shopping malls in Seoul – Coex Mall (see p100) and Times Square (see p104) are the only true malls in the city. However, there are department stores in every city district – the most notable are Shinsegae Department Store in Myeongdong (see p82) and Galleria in Apgujeong (see p104). There are lots of markets all over Seoul, the most famous ones being Dongdaemun and Namdaemun (for both, see p82). The former is the best place to buy fabric – some shop owners speak enough English to make by-the-meter sales, and international credit cards are usually accepted.

Apgujeong is Seoul's prime designer-label territory. Flagship stores of the main international brands dot Apgujeongno (see p101), the area's main road, while boutiques selling top local brands can be found on the side-streets toward Dosan Park. Finally, Insadong (see pp16–19) is the best place to head for goods such as pottery, tea sets, rice cakes, art supplies, and handmade paper.

Korea is famed for its electronic goods, though they may be no cheaper here than in your own country. Yongsan Electronics Market (see p58) and **Techno Mart** are Seoul's two main electronics malls.

All of Seoul's large bookstores have foreign-language sections. **Youngpoong** and **Kyobo** have good selections, but **What the Book?**, a large English-only store near Itaewon station, is by far the best.

When you buy a product bearing a "Tax-Free Shopping" label, you'll be able to claim a VAT refund at the airport when leaving the country. It is best to inquire about the details at the airport when you arrive in Seoul.

Where to Eat

The cuisine of Korea (see pp46–7) is highly distinctive. A lack of familiarity pushes some foreign travelers towards Western burgers, sandwiches, and pizza, but it would be a shame not to give Korean food a try – chances are you will love it.

The standard Korean meal revolves around rice and meat or fish, together with a soup and umpteen side-dishes – known as banchan, the latter are often the highlight of the meal. Koreans rarely dine alone, and most meals are made for sharing. This may seem alien to some visitors, but it certainly makes the dining experience a lot more fun, particularly with something like a barbecued meat feast. In group situations, just follow what the locals do. Although there are many rules of etiquette to obey, foreigners are usually forgiven any slips in this regard.

Most Korean meals are eaten with chopsticks, although foreigners may sometimes be provided with a fork. If you have never tried using chopsticks before, give it a go – most people pick it up fairly quickly, much to the surprise of the locals.

Korea isn't exactly a vegetarian's paradise. Although vegetables feature prominently in most meals (especially in the aforementioned banchan), few dishes are vegetarian only, and even those that are may have been prepared with the same utensils used for cooking meat.

While an admirable number of Seoul's restaurants have English-language menus, many at the cheaper end of the scale do not. Deciphering Korean menus is perhaps the fastest means of learning the local alphabet. With a little effort, it might not be as difficult as you expect.

Payment tends to take place on the way out of the restaurant. The highly Confucian nature of Korean society means that it is customary for hosts to pay, and locals rarely split the bill when eating with each other. However, they may offer to perform this task when eating with foreigners. The sight of foreign travelers bickering over who should pay what will likely elicit laughter from restaurant staff.

Tipping is another concept largely alien to Koreans – leave even a small bit of change in the hands of your waiter or waitress, and they'll probably chase you down the road in an effort to hand it back to you.

Where to Stay

The bulk of Seoul's best hotels are clustered around City Hall, to the north of the river, and Gangnam, to the south; the former is a bit more convenient for sightseeing. Facilities and services are as you would expect, though due to Seoul's huge population density, rooms tend to be a little smaller than the international norm.

Myeongdong district, near City Hall, is well located and has a profusion of motels (seedy, but usually fine for those on a budget) and mid-range hotels, while the student district of Hongdae is best for both nightlife and hostels.

Hongdae also has plenty of B&B-style accommodation, and some places are really quite nice.

Finally, but most excitingly, the Bukchon area has a dozen guesthouses set within wooden hanok houses, among the city's most traditional and charming places to stay.

DIRECTORY

NEWSPAPERS AND MAGAZINES

10 Magazine
w 10mag.com

Korea Herald
w koreaherald.com

Korea Times
w koreatimes.co.kr

TOURIST INFORMATION

Korea Tourism Organization
w english.visitkorea.or.kr
📞 02 1330

Seoul Tourism Organization
w visitseoul.net
📞 02 120

SHOPPING

Kyobo
MAP L4 ■ 1 Jongno

Techno Mart
MAP G4 ■ 546-4 Guui 3-dong

What The Book?
MAP R6 ■ 176-2 Itaewondong
w whatthebook.com

Youngpoong Bookstore
MAP M4 ■ 41 Cheonggyecheonno

Places to Stay

PRICE CATEGORIES
For a standard, double room per night (with breakfast if included), taxes and extra charges.

....

W under W100,000   **WW** W100,000–400,000
WWW over W400,000

Luxury Hotels

Fraser Suites
MAP N4 ▪ 272 Nakwondong ▪ 6262 8888 ▪ seoul.frasers hospitality.com ▪ WW
The best of Seoul's smattering of serviced residences – most guests are here for weeks or months, but shorter stays are also possible. Service is excellent, rooms are huge, and there is a rooftop golf driving range and an on-site swimming pool.

Grand Intercontinental Seoul Parnas
MAP F5 ▪ 521 Teheranno ▪ 555 5656 ▪ www.grand icparnas.com ▪ WW
Sprouting from the southern end of the COEX shopping complex, this already excellent hotel has looked even snazzier since a renovation in 2013. There are some superb restaurants on the lower floors, as well as an indoor pool.

JW Marriott
MAP D5 ▪ 19–3 Banpodong ▪ 6282 6262 ▪ www.marriott.com ▪ WW
A classy hotel that is conveniently located at a junction of three subway lines and Seoul's main bus terminal. The Marriott's amenities include a spa, fitness club, restaurant, and indoor pool. In addition, the upper floors offer excellent river views.

The Plaza
MAP L5 ▪ 119 Sogongno ▪ 771 2200 ▪ www.hotel theplaza.com ▪ WW
This top-quality hotel has a central location that overlooks City Hall and Seoul Plaza, and it includes amenities such as a spa and fitness center, as well as indoor swimming pool. Note that music events usually take place every summer evening on Seoul Plaza.

W Seoul Walkerhill
MAP D2 ▪ 21 Gwangjangdong ▪ 465 2222 ▪ www.wseoul.com ▪ WW
Aimed at 20- and 30-somethings, this hotel is a favorite with honeymooning Koreans. The snazzy rooms feature Jacuzzis, while the common areas include super-trendy bars and cafés.

Grand Hyatt
MAP S5 ▪ 322 Sowollo ▪ 797 1234 ▪ www.seoul. grand.hyatt.com ▪ WWW
Located partway up Namsan (see pp24–5), a mountain at the center of Seoul, this hotel offers a superb view of the city from most of its rooms and restaurants, all of which are top-drawer. There is also an excellent on-site bar, JJ Mahoney's (see p90).

Park Hyatt
MAP F6 ▪ 995–14 Daechidong ▪ 2016 1234 ▪ www.seoul.park. hyatt.com ▪ WWW
Guests will feel quite special when checking in at the top-floor reception of this stunning hotel – and this feeling is only magnified when moving to the rooms. All the designer bedrooms are decorated with compact, Zen-style furnishings.

Sheraton D Cube
MAP A4 ▪ 662 Gyeonginro ▪ 2211 2000 ▪ www.sheratonseoul dcubecity.co.kr ▪ WWW
Part of the stunning D Cube City complex, this 41-floor hotel is extremely well designed. There is an indoor pool, and a virtual Screen Golf Course and Driving Range, on the 27th floor. There is also a spa. The location is a little inconvenient for sightseeing, although it is ideal for those doing business in nearby Yeouido.

The Shilla
MAP D3 ▪ 202 Jangchungdong ▪ 2233 3131 ▪ www.shilla.net ▪ WWW
The most traditionally Korean of Seoul's five-star hotels, The Shilla is a real hit with overseas visitors. Both rooms and common areas are filled with charming accoutrements, and the hotel also has a spa.

The Westin Chosun
MAP L5 ▪ 87–1 Sogongdong ▪ 771 0500 ▪ www.echosunhotel.com ▪ WWW
South Korea's first top-end hotel is still one of its best. There are superb restaurants and facilities, and the helpful, well-trained staff are without equal in Seoul.

Mid-Range Hotels

Doulos Hotel
MAP N4 ▪ 112 Gwansudong ▪ 2266 2244 ▪ www.douloshotel.com ▪ W
This simple hotel is located in downtown Seoul. The guest rooms on offer are basic yet comfortable, and impeccably clean.

Gangnam Artnouveau City II
MAP D6 ▪ 1330–4 Seochodong ▪ 580 7500 ▪ www.artnouveaucity.co.kr ▪ W
The hotel's huge, richly decorated rooms are set in a serviced residence located on a fascinating Gangnam side-street. Substantial discounts on the rack rates are usually available, particularly for longer-term stays. The hotel has a fitness center, an Italian restaurant, and a garden on top of the building.

Ibis Myeongdong
MAP M6 ▪ 59–5 Myeongdong 1-ga ▪ 6361 8888 ▪ www.ibishotel.com ▪ W
Excellent customer service, great buffet breakfasts, and a highly accessible location more than compensate for the slightly small rooms at the Ibis Myengdong. The hotel offers guests a gym and a restaurant.

IP Boutique
MAP S5 ▪ 737–32 Hannamdong ▪ 3702 8000 ▪ www.ipboutiquehotel.com ▪ W
This hotel has more than 100 rooms, all designed with care. There is an on-site restaurant, and Itaewon's cosmopolitan array of eateries is only a short walk away.

Metro Hotel
MAP M5 ▪ 199–33 Euljiro 2-ga ▪ 752 1112 ▪ www.metrohotel.co.kr ▪ W
A splendid little mid-range hotel tucked into the Myeongdong shopping district. The rooms and service standards are far higher than you would expect at this price range, and there are hundreds of restaurants within a few minutes' walk. Breakfast is complimentary, and there's free Wi-Fi as well.

Seven Street
MAP N4 ▪ 125-1 Gwansudong ▪ 2278 8882 ▪ sutton-seoul.hotel-rn.com ▪ W
This is currently the city's only decent accommodation looking out onto Cheonggyecheon, the stream so beloved of visitors to Seoul. Guests will also be minutes from Tapgol Park and close to Gyeongbok Palace.

Yoido
MAP A4 ▪ 10–3 Yeouidodong ▪ 782 0121 ▪ www.yoidohotel.co.kr ▪ W
This is an affordable option in the Yeouido business district. The rooms are very good value for the price, there is a 24-hour fitness center, and the delightful Han riverside – great for a stroll – is just a stone's throw away.

PJ Hotel
MAP P5 ▪ 73–1 Inhyeondong ▪ 2280 7000 ▪ www.hotelpj.co.kr ▪ WW
PJ Hotel is hugely popular with Japanese visitors to Seoul, meaning that excellent customer service and sky-high standards of cleanliness prevail. There are two restaurants and a café in the hotel. Wi-Fi access is free for guests, and there is also a women-only floor.

Prince Hotel
MAP D3 ▪ 1–1 Namsandong 2-ga ▪ 752 7111 ▪ www.hotelprinceseoul.co.kr ▪ WW
A smart hotel with a great location – just across the road from the busy Myeongdong shopping district, though without the bustle. There is a range of color-coordinated rooms to choose from, and a coffee shop with a lounge.

Royal Hotel
MAP D2 ▪ 6–3 Myeongdong 1-ga ▪ 756 1112 ▪ www.royal.co.kr ▪ WW
Positioned at the upper end of mid-range, the Royal Hotel offers beautifully decorated rooms, and a plethora of shopping and dining opportunities right on its doorstep. The hotel also has a spa, bar, and restaurant.

Traditional Hanok

Anguk Guesthouse
MAP M2 ■ 72–3
Angukdong ■ 736 8304
■ www.anguk-house.com
■ W

Upon request, the gracious owners will pick you up from Anguk subway station, since their guesthouse can be hard to track. Guests are offered a range of delicious teas and, unlike in some other *hanok* options, there are Western-style beds in the rooms.

Bukchon Guesthouse
MAP M2 ■ 72 Gyedong
■ 010 6711 6717 ■ www.bukchon72.com ■ W

A collection of three small guesthouses, which together provide a wide range of rooms – some small, some fairly large.

Bukchon Maru
MAP N1 ■ 152 Changdeokgunggil
■ 744 8751 ■ www.bukchon maru.com ■ W

This charming guesthouse is run by a family who've been in the Bukchon area for decades – in fact, it was the owner's childhood home. The breakfasts are something you'll enjoy waking up to.

Dam Sojung
MAP M1 ■ 57 Gahoedong
■ 3749 9550 ■ W

A small garden welcomes guests of this 100-year old *hanok* as it strives to recreate an authentic experience. The home cooking is also excellent – enjoy *bibimbap* and other traditional Korean dishes.

Hanok Homestay
2148 1855 ■ homestay.jongno.go.kr ■ W

A wonderful program giving visitors the chance to stay with residents of the neighborhood. Properties vary in quality, but owners are almost uniformly friendly, with a real desire to introduce Korean culture to visitors.

Midam Guesthouse
MAP M2 ■ 79–10 Gyedong
■ 010 3143 7096 ■ www.midamhouse.com ■ W

Midam is a traditional guesthouse with four guest rooms and separate toilets for each one. There's a kitchen to cook in if desired and breakfast is provided free of charge from 8 to 10am. Coffee is free as well.

Rakkojae
MAP M2 ■ 99–2 Gyedong
■ 742 3410 ■ www.rkj.co.kr ■ W

This elegant option has beautifully manicured gardens and gorgeous period furniture, and it serves traditional meals and tea – all in a genuine 1870s *hanok*. However, the owners are not always accommodating, and the rooms can be overpriced for what they are.

Sophia Guesthouse
MAP L2 ■ 157–1 Sogyeokdong ■ 720 7220 ■ W

Dating from the 1860s, this is the oldest *hanok* guesthouse in the area. The rooms, which surround a pretty, shaded courtyard, are suitably traditional in feel and are superbly decorated. Public transport is readily available from here.

Sopoong
MAP K2 ■ 7-6 Tonguidong ■ 010 8998 9159 ■ www.facebook.com/sopoong.guesthouse ■ W

One of the smallest guesthouses in the area, this place has just four rooms. The manager is renowned for helping each and every guest get the most from their stay in Seoul.

Tea Guesthouse
MAP M2 ■ 131–1 Gyedong
■ 3675 9877 ■ www.tea guesthouse.com ■ W

Rooms here are modern by *hanok* standards, and have TVs and computers with Internet access. The common areas, however, are traditional, with gorgeous folding screens, period furniture, and decorative walls. Small tea ceremonies are also held here.

Yoo's Family Guesthouse
MAP N2 ■ 156 Gwonnongdong ■ 3673 3266 ■ www.yoosfamily.com ■ W

The owners make great efforts to please international guests, making this the friendliest *hanok* option in the area. They have two locations in a wonderful area, just to the west of the Jongmyo shrine (see p27).

Myeonggajae
MAP M1 ■ 79–12 Gahoedong ■ 9880 6979 ■ www.myeonggajae.com ■ WW

The special thing about Myeonggajae is that you can only reserve the whole guesthouse (three rooms and two bathrooms) - perfect for families, large groups, or anybody who doesn't want to be disturbed by unfamiliar faces.

Budget Stays

2nd Casa Hotel
MAP M5 ▪ 335–2 Euljiro 3-ga ▪ 2266 1553 ▪ www.2ndcasa.com ▪ W
A simple hotel, 2nd Casa is tucked into the old-fashioned, but highly atmospheric, side-streets off Euljiro. It has the feel of a youth hostel – albeit one with clean, private rooms. The location is also a plus as it is merely a 5 to 10 minute walk from all major tourist attractions.

Hide & Seek
MAP K2 ▪ 35-68 Tonguidong ▪ 6925 5916 ▪ www.hidenseek. co.kr ▪ W
Hide & Seek is a quirky place that defies simple explanation – this is a boutique guesthouse set in a Japanese Colonial-era mansion, with sun-beds on the roof, a lobby that looks like an art gallery, and a wonderful family-style breakfast laid out every morning in the café downstairs.

Hotel 648
MAP F5 ▪ 648–7 Yeoksamdong ▪ 553 4737 ▪ www.648hotel.co.kr ▪ W
While most of Seoul's love motels hide behind a wafer-thin veneer of respectability, this one is proud of its purpose – ironically, this has made it popular with travelers as well. Each room has been jazzed up with a Jacuzzi, mirror-tiling and the like, while some have heart-shaped beds.

Hotel D'Oro
MAP R5 ▪ 124–3 Itaewondong ▪ 749 6525 ▪ W
This affordable Itaewon option is situated off the main street, far enough to eliminate almost all of the noise from passing traffic. The rooms here are surprisingly clean for the area, and at this price level the Hotel D'Oro stands out as one of the best options in the area.

Hotel M
MAP A4 ▪ 14–23 Yeouidodong ▪ 783 2271 ▪ www.hotelm.co.kr ▪ W
A good business hotel, the M offers large, clean rooms designed along five different color schemes. All of the private bathrooms have excellent power showers, and some also have small whirlpool bathtubs. The hotel also has a chic on-site café-bar.

J-Hill
MAP M6 ▪ 33–1 Myeongdong ▪ 753 8900 ▪ www.jhill.kr ▪ W
A relative newbie in the Myeongdong area, J-Hill is a great choice. The rooms may be on the small side, but the staff are amiable and helpful, and the breakfasts fantastic. There's also a viewing balcony – a brilliant place to have a cup of coffee.

Sunbee
MAP M3 ▪ 198–11 Gwanhundong ▪ 730 3451 ▪ W
Though a little old-fashioned for some, Sunbee is easy on the budget. Rooms contain everything you're likely to need during your

stay in Seoul, as well as some extras such as hairdryers, toiletries, and cable TV.

Templestay
MAP M3 ▪ 56 Ujeongguk-ro ▪ 2031 2000 ▪ eng. templestay.com ▪ W
A unique cultural program, Templestay enables foreign visitors to spend the night at temples across South Korea and experience the life of Buddhist practitioners. Bongeunsa (see p99) and Jogyesa (see p16) are among the various temples in Seoul that are a part of this program. Note that the temples serve only vegetarian food, and guests have to wake up early to take part in temple routines.

Tria
MAP F5 ▪ 677–11 Yeoksamdong ▪ 553 2471 ▪ www.triahotel. co.kr ▪ W
A south-of-the-river hotel, the Tria offers rooms that are astonishingly well designed for the price. Suites don't cost much more than the regular rooms. There's also a trendy on-site bar.

Urbanwood
MAP S1 ▪ 5 Wausanno 29-gil ▪ 070 8613 0062 ▪ www.urbanwood.co.kr ▪ W
The nicest of the myriad homestay-style guesthouses to have opened up in Hongdae in recent years, Urbanwood has pretty rooms, a view from the rooftop, and an owner who makes some of the best espresso in Seoul.

For a key to hotel price categories see p114

Index

Acknowledgments

Author

Martin Zatko is a travel writer and consultant specializing in East Asia. He has written almost two dozen travel guides, including half a dozen about the Korean peninsula. He first visited Seoul in 2002, just before the World Cup came to town, and the city has been a home away from home for him ever since.

Publishing Director Georgina Dee

Publisher Vivien Antwi

Design Director Phil Ormerod

Editorial Ankita Awasthi Troger, Michelle Crane, Rachel Fox, Freddie Marriage, Akshay Rana, Sally Schafer, Sands Publishing Solutions, Rachel Thompson

Design Tessa Bindloss, Richard Czapnik, Bhavika Mathur, Marisa Renzullo

Commissioned Photography Rough Guides/Martin Richardson, James Tye

Picture Research Ellen Root, Lucy Sienkowska, Rituraj Singh

Cartography Subhashree Bharti, Suresh Kumar, James Macdonald, Sachin Pradhan

DTP Jason Little, George Nimmo

Production Poppy Werder-Harris

Factchecker Won Jang

Proofreader Leena Lane

Indexer Hilary Bird

Picture Credits

The publisher would like to thank the following for their kind permission to reproduce their photographs:
Key: a-above; b-below/bottom; c-centre; f-far; l-left; r-right; t-top

123RF.com: Nattee Chalermtiragool 23cr; Ping Han 23tl; Ivan Marchuk 41cr, 78b; siraphol 65b; Siraphol Siricharattakul 22bl; Sung Kuk Kim 19b; vincentstthomas 18t; Tan Kian Yong 28cl.

4Corners: Massimo Borchi 23br.

74: 55tr, 102bl.

Alamy Stock Photo: Cecilia Colussi 44tl; Wendy Connett 18c; dbimages / Derek Brown 30br, / Jeremy Graham 39br; Elena Ermakova 2tr; 36-7; Michelle Gilders 16bl; hemis.fr/Ludovic Maisant 20cr, 54t, 97cla; MarioPonta 92tl, 94c; Simon Reddy 46br; searagen 1, 84-5; SFL Travel 72br; Dave Tacon 50tl; khanh nghia tran 4cl; World History Archive 38br; Yooniq Images 4t, 7tr, 11cr, 21cl, 21crb, 24clb, 29bl, 34-5, 35crb; Yooniqlmages 10crb, 43tr, 51tr, 100tl.

All That Jazz: 90clb.

Arario Gallery: 14cb.

AWL Images: Travel Pix Collection 16-7.

Bridgeman Images: 38cl; National Museum of Korea 21ca.

Corbis: 2/Multi-bits/Ocean 57tr; Atlantide Phototravel/Massimo Borchi 43b, 61tr, 62t, 99cr; Tibor Bognar 86tl; Godong/Pascal Deloche 95cla; JAI/ Christian Kober 20cl, / Jane Sweeney 25crb, 68tl; Photononstop/ Calle Montes 11ca; Jane Sweeney 71cl; Topic Photo Agency 10b, 16cl, 33br, 34cl, 40tl, 47cl, 65tr, 93br, 94b, /Young Teck Hong 10c.

Craftworks Taphouse: 56br.

Dreamstime.com: Amadeustx 26-7, 60tl; Barbarico 28-9, 34br; Robert Paul Van Beets 30-1; F11photo 6l, 25bl; Firststar 7cr; Goncharov2006 42bl; Hanhanpeggy 48t, 62bl; Hlphoto 47tr; Imkenneth 61cl, 76cr; Ixuskmitl 3tr, 32br, 69t, 106-7; Jackbluee 87tr; Junyan Jiang 75crb; Joymsk 78cl; Le Cong Duc Dao 46cr; Longtaildog 4cr; Cj Nattanai 24-5, 70cl, 101cla; Nattanai 80tr; Nisarabee 64clb; Nyker1 2tl, 8-9; Ongchangwei 77t; Christian Papainog 27clb; Sean Pavone 3tl, 4crb, 66-7; Pigprox 80bl; Tanawat Pontchour 32cl; Prakobkit 63cl; Tawatchai Prakobkit 4cla, 4b, 29crb, 52-3, 70b, 100b; Artaporn Puthikampol 69br; Reika7 47tl; Jordan Tan 13ca, 26bl, 33tl; Thejipen 72tl; Vincentstthomas 11crb, 12-3, 27ca, 98ca; Jess Yu 93t, 97crb.

Dugahun: 75cla.

Galleria: 58br.

Gallery Factory: Hong Cheolki 15cl.

Gana Art Gallery: 11clb.

Getty Images: Insung Choi 44b; Gavin Hellier 19tr; Izzet Keribar 10l; Sungjin Kim 32-3; The LIFE Picture Collection/Francis Miller 39tl; Light of Peace 45cr; Lonely Planet 19cla; Martin Moos 29clb; Chinnaphong Mungsiri 45tl; ilgan sport 89cl; Chung Sung-Jun 63tr.

Grand Hyatt Seoul: 90tr.

Park Hyatt Seoul: 54bl, 102tr, 105t.

iStockphoto.com: Min-Gyu Seong 12br; Tuangtong 11tr; whitewish 46tl.

Kukje Gallery: 14tl, 60br.

Kwang Ju Yo: 33clb, 74b.

Hotel Lotte Co., Ltd: 56tl, 81cr, 83t.

Melting Shop: 103cr.

National Folk Museum of Korea: 13br.

National Palace Museum of Korea: 15b, 40-1.

Stephan Oberteufer: 96t.

Rex by Shutterstock: Seong Joon Cho 48br;

Colorsport 39cl.

Robert Harding Picture Library: Tibor Bognar 104cl; Jose Fuste Raga 22-3, 42tr; Godong 4clb; Christian Kober 88b.

Seokparang: 73cla.

Seoul Museum of Art: 41tr; Seoul Babel 79cl.

Ssamzigil: 59cr.

SuperStock: age fotostock/Pietro Scozzari 51cl, /Wendy Connett 18br.

Tour Seoul <visitseoul.net>: 82br; 87b.

Yido Pottery: 58t.

Cover

Front and spine: **AWL Images:** Travel Pix Collection

Back: **Dreamstime.com:** Sepavo

Pull Out Map Cover

AWL Images: Travel Pix Collection

All other images © Dorling Kindersley
For further information see:
www.dkimages.com

Penguin
Random
House

Printed and bound in China

First published in the United States in 2013
by Dorling Kindersley Limited
345 Hudson Street, New York,
New York 10014

Copyright 2013, 2017 © Dorling
Kindersley Limited

A Penguin Random House Company

17 18 19 20 10 9 8 7 6 5 4 3 2 1

Reprinted with revisions 2015, 2017

A CIP catalogue record is available from the British Library.

ISSN 1479-344X

ISBN 978 1 4654 5997 8

MIX
Paper from
responsible sources
FSC™ C018179

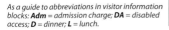

*As a guide to abbreviations in visitor information blocks: **Adm** = admission charge; **DA** = disabled access; **D** = dinner; **L** = lunch.*

Phrase Book

The Korean language uses an alphabet called Hangeul. Pronouncing Korean words is a tough task – some sounds simply do not have English-language equivalents. For example, there's only one character for "l" and "r," with the sound somewhere in between the two. The letters "k," "d," "b," and "j" are often written "k," "t," "p," and "ch," and are pronounced approximately halfway towards those Roman equivalents. Consonants are fairly easy to master – note that some are doubled up, and spoken more forcefully. See the Guidelienes for Pronunciation for some of the tricky vowels and diphthongs (British English readings offer the closest equivalents).

Guidelines for Pronunciation: Consonants

Note that some consonants are pronounced differently depending upon whether they start or finish a syllable. In these cases, the terminal readings have been given in parentheses.

ㄱ	g (k)	ㅗ	o
ㄴ	n	ㅛ	yo
ㄷ	d (t)	ㅜ	u
ㄹ	r/l	ㅠ	yu
ㅁ	m	ㅡ	eu
ㅂ	b (p)	ㅣ	i
ㅅ	s (t)	ㅔ	e
ㅈ	j (t)	ㅐ	ae
ㅊ	ch (t)	ㅖ	ye
ㅋ	k	ㅒ	yae
ㅌ	t	ㅟ	wi
ㅍ	p	ㅞ	we
ㅎ	h	ㅙ	wae
ㅇ	ng	ㅘ	wa
ㅏ	a	ㅚ	oe
ㅑ	ya	ㅢ	ui
ㅓ	eo	ㅝ	wo
ㅕ	yeo		

Vowels

a	as in "car"
ya	as in "yap"
eo	as in "hot"
yeo	as in "yob"
o	pronounced "ore"
yo	pronounced as "your"
u	as in "Jew"
yu	pronounced "you"
eu	no English equivalent; widen your mouth and try an "euggh" sound of disgust
i	as in "pea"

Useful Phrases

Yes	ye/ne	예/네
No	aniyo	아니요
Please (asking for something)	…juseyo	…주세요
Excuse me	shillye hamnida	실례합니다
I'm sorry	mian hamnida	미안합니다
Thank you	gamsa hamnida	감사합니다
Do you speak English?	yeongeo halsu-isseoyo?	영어 할 수 있어요?
Is there someone who can speak English?	yeongeo-reul haljul a-neun bun isseoyo?	영어를 할 줄 아는 분 있어요?

I can't speak Korean	jeo-neun hangugeo-reul mot haeyo	저는 한국어를 못 해요
Please help me	dowa-juseyo	도와 주세요
Hello; Good morning/ afternoon/evening	annyeong haseyo	안녕 하세요
Hello (polite)	annyeong hashimnikka	안녕 하십니까
How are you?	jal jinaesseoyo?	잘 지냈어요?
I'm fine	jal jinaesseoyo /jo-ayo	잘 지냈어요 / 좋아요

Directions and Places

Where is (x)?	-i/ga eodi-eyo?	-이/가 어디에 요?
Straight ahead	jikjin	직진
Left	oen-jjok (pronounced "wen-chok")	왼쪽
Right	oreun-jjok	오른쪽
Behind	dwi-ae	뒤에
In front of	ap-ae	앞에
Map	maep/jido	맵/지도
Entrance	ip-gu	입구
Exit	chul-gu	출구
Museum	bangmulgwan	박물관
Park	gongwon	공원
Temple	Jeol/sachal	절/사찰
Toilet	hwajang-shil	화장실
Tourist office	gwan-gwang annaeso	관광 안내소

Staying in a Hotel

Hotel	hotel	호텔
Motel	motel	모텔
Guesthouse	yeogwan	여관
Budget guesthouse	yeoinsuk	여인숙
Rented room	minbak	민박
Youth hostel	yuseu hoseutel	유스 호스텔
Korean-style room	ondol-bang	온돌방
Western-style room	chimdae-bang	침대방
Single room	shinggeul chimdae	싱글 침대
Double room	deobeul chimdae	더블 침대
Twin room	chimdae dugae	침대 두 개
En-suite room	yokshil-ddallin bang	욕실 딸린방
Shower	syaweo	샤워
Bath	yokjo	욕조
Key	ki/yeol sae	키/열쇠
Passport	yeogwon	여권
Do you have any vacancies?	bang isseoyo?	방 있 어요?
How much is the room?	bang-i eolma -eyo?	방이 얼마에요?
Does that include breakfast?	gagyeok-e achim-shiksa poham-dwae isseoyo?	가격에 아침식사 포함돼 있는요?
I have a reservation	jeo-neun yeyak haesseoyo	저는 예약 했어요
I don't have a reservation	jeo-neun yeyak anhaesseoyo	저는 예약 안했어요
One/two/ three nights	haru/ iteol/ samil + bam	하룻밤/이틀밤 /삼일밤